PRESSING

QUESTIONS

A COLLECTION OF POLITICAL, ECONOMIC & LEGAL PERSPECTIVES

Contributors

Anthony Davies

Frederick Motson

Matthew Proud

Dinesh C. Rajp

The Earl of Caithness, Malcolm Ian Sinclair

John Tomlinson

Editor

Frederick Motson

authorHOUSE®

AuthorHouse™ UK Ltd.
500 Avebury Boulevard
Central Milton Keynes, MK9 2BE
www.authorhouse.co.uk
Phone: 08001974150

First published by AuthorHouse 2/23/2010

ISBN: 978-1-4490-6073-2 (sc)

This book is printed on acid-free paper.

Contents

Introduction

In any collection of compositions by different authors there arises the danger that the works chosen will either be repetitively similar in tone, or on the contrary that too eclectic a mix will lead to a collection with no unique voice or guiding principle. It is my hope that this volume has plotted a course between these two extremes. While there is a diverse selection of authors, ranging from the economist John Tomlinson through lawyers and academics to The Earl of Caithness, who remains an active politician, there is a theme which emerges from each article, extract or speech.

Whether it is Anthony Davies discussing the judicial and governmental decisions which have led the way for those interned at Guantanamo Bay detention camp to exercise their legal rights, or Dinesh Rajp developing new perspectives on the influence of culture in the post-colonial world, all of the compositions in this publication deal with issues which impact on modern society, from the highest levels of governance to the man on the Clapham (or indeed the Copenhagen, Cairo or Caracas) omnibus.

There is also a strong emphasis on not only recognising and identifying issues such as national security, financial regulation and human rights, but also on suggesting solutions and stimulating reasoned debate. It is for this reason that certain articles written some time ago are included 'as is' - most notably 'Honest money', which is illuminating in highlighting problems with our financial system that were left to cause crisis again in 2008.

I hope that the following will not only prove interesting, but also stimulating and in the most constructive sense, contentious enough to inspire debate.

Frederick Motson
London, September 2009

Contributors

John Tomlinson

John Tomlinson was born in Canada and studied business administration at Florida State University in the United States. He practiced as a stockbroker with Thomson & McKinnon, a member of the New York Stock Exchange, before he married an English woman and came to live in the United Kingdom.

Having studied the effect of debt on the economies of developed and less developed countries, he set up, and is Chairman of, Oxford Research and Development Corporation Limited which explores the use of equity instruments and the development of equity markets for areas of finance currently served by debt.

John now resides in the Algarve region of Portugal, where he divides his time between writing and sailing on his ship Malaika, around the Mediterranean.

The Earl of Caithness, Malcolm Ian Sinclair

Having attended the Royal Agricultural College, Cirencester, Malcolm Sinclair worked for a firm of land agents in Oxfordshire. That led him into commercial agency and in 1984 Mrs Margaret Thatcher, the Prime Minister, invited him to join her reforming government. He started as a Whip and Lord in Waiting to The Queen before progressing to an Under Secretary of State at the Department of Transport and then

Minister of State at, successively, the Home Office, Department of the Environment, the Treasury, the Foreign and Commonwealth Office and back to the Department of Transport. He is the only hereditary peer last century to have served in the three great Departments of State and while in the Treasury was also Paymaster General. He was created a Privy Councillor to Her Majesty The Queen in 1990.

Since 1994 he has undertaken consultancy work for various companies and jointly founded Victoria Soames Ltd., and a London real estate agency. As one of the 90 remaining hereditary peers he also still takes an active part in politics from the backbenches in Parliament as well as serving on the European sub-committee considering legislation from Brussels on Agricultural and Environmental matters. He is also involved with heritage and charity work in the north of Scotland.

Frederick Motson

Frederick Motson studied Law & Politics at the University of Buckingham, where he achieved the Edgar Palamountain Award for Excellence, graduating at the top of his year. He has a keen interest in politics and continues to write on the area despite having chosen the law as a profession.

A member of Grays Inn, he was called to the Bar in October 2008. He currently teaches Law at the University of Westminster, London. Frederick also reports judgments for the Consumer and Trading Law Cases law reports.

Anthony Davies

After serving for many years in the Royal Navy Anthony turned his attention to academia; first, completing his Bachelor of Law degree; secondly, an LL.M degree in commercial and international law with a further designation as a international law specialist; and finally, undertaking the legal practice course at the Oxford Institute of Legal Practice. Currently, he is working at a major Oxford-based law firm.

Matthew W. Proud

Matthew Proud is an international law specialist, based in London, England, who primarily focuses on Human Rights issues in Hong Kong.

After completing his Bachelor of Laws with Honours he went on to complete a Masters degree in Law at the University of Buckingham, during which time he conducted empirical research in Hong Kong. Additionally, Matthew has a keen interest in the area of law surrounding the judicial review of unincorporated associations, under the Human Rights Act.

Matthew is currently undertaking the vocational stage of his legal training at City University London, formerly the Inns of Court School of Law, to become a barrister.

Dinesh C. Rajp

Dinesh Rajp began his career in banking, working first in foreign currency trading and then in small business management. After founding his own business consultancy company he became increasingly interested in the law and achieved his bachelor's degree and a Master's degree by way of research at the University of Buckingham.

He is currently a lecturer in law at the University of Westminster, also teaching in the ILEX programme. His research specialisations lie in human rights and international law.

HONEST MONEY – A CHALLENGE TO BANKING

By John Tomlinson

Editor's note: First published in 1993 John Tomlinson's work is a reminder of the failure to recognise, limit or regulate prolificacy in international finance prior to the current economic downturn

The Mechanics of Misrepresentation

A hundred years ago, a Mr Goldsmith opened Anybank. His first depositor, Mr Sure, came in to lodge a gold coin for safekeeping. Mr Goldsmith gave him a receipt. Mr Short then came in, to borrow a gold coin, to buy a horse from Mr Trainer. In exchange for his horse, Mr Trainer accepted the gold coin from Mr Short. He took it to Anybank, and lodged it with Mr Goldsmith, who gave him a receipt. A normal set of transactions when the gold standard existed.

The strange thing about this story, however, is that Mr Goldsmith had issued two receipts, yet he had only one gold coin. Both receipts were available for use in the market-place. Yet only one gold coin actually existed against which Mr Trainer and Mr Sure could validly claim. The market-place will, therefore, have been led to believe that there was one more gold coin in existence than there was in reality. So the mechanisms of misrepresentation are created.

1

Let me take you back to the beginning of banking, to see better how this came about. Our present system is a direct descendant from the money-lending practices of the early goldsmiths. Suppose we were back in the days when trade was in its infancy, and the gold standard was just beginning, and you had some gold you wished to store. You would have several choices.

You could keep it on your person at all times: with one gold coin this would pose no serious risk. If, on the other hand, you were a wealthy goldsmith, who had large quantities of gold to store, you might require and could, perhaps, afford to build a strong-room. But, if you were in the middle, and had too much gold to carry with you at all times, but not enough to warrant constructing your own strong-box or strong-room, you might well choose to arrange with a goldsmith to store your gold on one of the shelves in his strong-room. (In those days a shelf was known as a 'bank', hence the derivation of today's word.) The goldsmith concerned would then issue you with a receipt: a valid claim against your portion of the gold in that goldsmith's strong-room.

This, of course, is what happened historically. It was, then, a natural step for holders of goldsmiths' receipts to begin to use them in exchanges, rather than using gold itself. It avoided the risk of carrying gold to the marketplace. To facilitate trade the goldsmiths - or "bankers" as they became known - began to issue standard receipts for specified amounts of gold. These receipts were issued for amounts known commonly to be used in exchanges. So, when anyone took his gold to be stored he would be given a number of small value receipts for it.

The integrity of the banker was crucial to the acceptance of these receipts: the banker had to intend to, and be able to, honour each receipt. If he had issued receipts for more gold than he possessed, he would be unable to honour all the receipts issued. Some holders of his receipts would then not be able to retrieve the gold they claimed, or all would receive less than the full value of their receipts.

No paper claim or receipt is valid without this fundamental relationship.

If the gold is not there, then the face value of the paper becomes irrelevant. Similarly, if the issuer's intent is suspect, then so is the claim, and that suspicion will be reflected in the way that the market-place receives his receipts.

Invalid claims

Yet there are many factors which can cause a goldsmith's receipt to be worth less than it claims to be. One is a robbery. Robbery will result in insufficient gold to meet all claims. Genuine robbery cannot be held to be the goldsmith's fault. There are, however, four factors which can be a result of the goldsmith's deliberate actions:

1. The goldsmith might have created receipts against which no gold had been received, and used for them personal exchanges in the market-place.

2. He could have used some of the gold, against which receipts had already been issued, for personal exchanges in the market-place.

3. He could have created receipts against which no gold had been received, and lent these receipts to someone else.

4. He could have lent somebody else some of the gold against which receipts had already been issued.

Each of these actions would clearly have led to an imbalance between the amount of gold actually available to honour receipts and the amount for which receipts had been issued. In each of these cases, the action of the goldsmith would have been self-serving and deliberate. No doubt some goldsmiths tried each.

The difficulty, of course, lies in knowing when they do it. If one has no access to the goldsmith's accounts, changes in the goldsmith's personal spending patterns would be the only indication that he might be using the client's gold for personal benefit. Depositors, therefore, had to remain alert to spot any significant changes in a goldsmith's lifestyle. Should any such change cause a doubt to arise, the only way of proving the goldsmith's ability to meet his issue is for all of his receipts to be presented at the same time. If they are honoured, his good faith will be proven.

Loans, however, have always been treated as confidential matters. It is not as easy, therefore, to observe the changes in a goldsmith's behaviour when he is using other people's gold to make loans, or lending receipts created without a gold deposit behind them. Such arrangements would only be of direct concern to the borrower and the goldsmith. Provided that the goldsmith behaved in a very circumspect manner, the only immediate change in consumption patterns would be in those of the borrower. (To avoid runs on their deposits which might test their ability to meet all of the receipts which they had issued, goldsmiths and their descendants, now known as bankers, have cultivated a reputation for circumspect and prudent behaviour.) The goldsmith would, however, have both betrayed trust and directly benefited.

Lending lies at the heart of current misrepresentation. The pattern of effects which flows from the practice of money-lending can be very insidious indeed. The practice itself warrants closer examination.

One of the most immediate effects of lending is that the market-place is led to believe - unjustifiably - that there is more gold available to serve its needs. If we look again at what happened when Mr Short wanted to buy a horse, Mr Trainer and Mr Sure each held a separate receipt against the same gold coin: a misrepresentation of fact. This misrepresentation is obscured by a normal accounting practice:

Deposits:	2 gold coins	*Cash:*	1 gold coin
			1 gold coin
	2 gold coins		2 gold coins

The books would thus have appeared to balance, whereas in reality Mr Goldsmith would have issued receipts for one more gold coin than in fact he had. This imbalance would have been clearly identified had the accounts read:

Receipts issued: <u>2 gold coins</u>

Stock in hand: <u>1 gold coin</u>

The nature of any collateral held by the bank is irrelevant. Whatever it is, it will not be a gold coin, or the loan would not have been necessary. Nor can it become a gold coin. At most it can be exchanged for a gold coin. But an exchange does not produce another coin. It merely changes ownership of an existing coin.

So, it is clear that a fault exists in the money-lending function of the banking system. The very mechanics of the lending process produces misrepresentation: it is dishonest. Yet it has become an accepted practice. It has been legitimised.

Invalid Claims Made Legitimate

A man in New Jersey once tried to corner the soybean oil market using a practice not dissimilar to that employed in the normal course of banking. He bought and paid for a storage tank of soybean oil. He then asked his bankers to test it for quantity and quality. He borrowed against it and bought a futures contract for the delivery of an equal amount of oil to him at some future date. He then shifted the oil to another tank and filled the first tank with water so that it would continue to appear full. He was not concerned about his borrowings, they had been covered by the futures contract.

He then had his bankers test the new tank for quality and quantity and borrowed against the new tank. He bought a further futures contract. He kept repeating the process in the hope of gaining control of the market and driving up its price to his advantage.

In each case, he had removed the real oil, and had effectively replaced it with a legal promise to deliver an equal amount of oil at some stage in the future. This is what the banking system does with our deposits. They are removed. Loan agreements are held in their stead. Loan agreements are agreements to deliver a specific amount of money to the lender at some future date.

The soybean oil man was eventually exposed. He was tried and convicted. He went to jail for fraud. Yet bankers, who in essence do the same thing with money, continue to function as legitimate businessmen - and, in fact, they are. Their misrepresentation has been legitimised. The legitimisation occurred so long ago that most, if not all, current bankers and customers have no knowledge of it. Today, bankers are seen as the pillars of the community. No reputable economist or financial expert of whom I am aware has questioned the validity of the money-lending mechanism of the banking system. To each it is a "given".

One of the most odious effects of this misrepresentation occurs when bankers voice their objections to wage rises, arguing that such rises are inflationary. Such comments are an insult to working people. Wage earners request a wage increase to claw back the purchasing power which has been removed from their pay packets. For reasons they do not fully understand, their wages can no longer adequately support their standard of living. Demands for higher pay lead to conflict and industrial dispute. Once again we can see how dishonest money divides decent people and sets man against man.

Then we hear financiers and bankers weigh in with arguments about the workers' greed. Yet we can now see that it is not workers' reed. It is the actions of bankers themselves that are causing the losses. The injustice of their comments is appalling.

Inverted logic

As we saw with the gold coin in the previous chapter, the system produced by superimposing the mechanism of money-lending onto the system for storing and distributing money is dishonest. It ought not to have the support of the legal system. Giving legal respectability to misrepresentation turns logic on its head. The widespread use and acceptance of institutionalised money-lending leads us to believe it is a sound practice. But it is based upon misrepresentation. It is dishonest. It certainly ought not to have the support of the legal system.

Nevertheless, it does have the support of the legal system, and the amount of the misrepresentation continues to grow. The amount can be measured. In a given banking system, it will equal the amount of loans outstanding on the books of all branches of all the banks in that particular system, less the paid-up capital of those banks. Each time the banking system as a whole produces a net increase in loans, the amount of misrepresentation will increase, and the real exchange value of each previously existing unit of money will decrease proportionately.

This decrease should become immediately apparent in the market-place - but it doesn't. Under the gold standard, for instance, prices remained stable during periods when misrepresentation was continually occurring. Hidden from public view, a gap was opening between the amount of gold available to honour claims and the amount of those claims. With each new misrepresentation the gap widened. Holders of claims were unaware of it. They believed that the claims which they held could be exchanged at any time for the amount of gold stated. So long as this view held, each claim was treated as if it were the amount of gold stated.

Confidence then became the key to successful banking. It was irrelevant that a bank could not meet all its issued claims if presented for payment at the same time. What mattered was that individual claims could be met when presented. Systems were put in place to assure depositors that their deposits were safe. The presence of these systems allowed lenders to increase their misrepresentation with impunity. Nevertheless, with the increased misrepresentation, prices remained stable.

Gold had a minimum exchange value. It was in demand as the principal medium of exchange and store of value for future exchanges; it was rare: it was hard to find: it required a considerable amount of expenditure of human energy for both its discovery and its production. People would not produce it for less than the effort to produce it was worth. If demand fell and its value in exchanges fell, less would be produced. As less was produced, less would be available to service the needs of the market-place, and its exchange value would begin to increase. These factors helped to provide a minimum level below which even massive misrepresentation could not push the exchange value of gold.

As a result, there was also a minimum exchange value below which claims on gold could not be pushed unless and until holders recognised that each claim could not be exchanged for the amount of gold stated on its face. Only then would the exchange value of paper claims collapse.

This prospect faced the Western monetary and banking system in the 1930's. Had the invalid claims then been declared illegitimate, the exchange value of gold would have risen as the market recognised that there was not nearly as large a supply as had been represented. As the exchange value of gold, or money as it was then, increased less of it would have been needed in exchanges for the same previous value of goods and services. Prices would have fallen. The holders of gold and valid claims would have found their purchasing power increased. The existing amount of gold would then have been able to support an increased volume of exchanges. This was not allowed to happen. Instead, the invalid claims were legitimised, and gold was removed as a form of money.

The problems faced by the monetary authorities and banking systems in the late 1920's and 1930's were a direct result of the practice of money-lending. In the United Kingdom, for instance, up to that time, a pound was the name given to a note which had a legal claim upon one quarter of an ounce of gold. Pound notes were issued both by private banks and the Bank of England. Each accepted pound notes as deposits as if they were gold itself. Each loaned both. The acceptance of pound notes as deposits, the issuance of receipts against them, and their eventual use for loans, merely served to compound the rate of misrepresentation. The mechanics of money-lending were misrepresenting both the amount of gold in the market-place and the amount of valid claims which were issued against gold.

It took a long time before a sufficient number of individuals began to suspect that they might not be able to exchange their claims for the exact amount of gold stated. During that long period, the exchange rate of both gold and claims remained very stable at, or near, the minimum level below which gold could not be pushed. When sufficient individuals did suspect the truth of the matter, they acted with natural self-interest. The suspicious preferred not to hold notes for future exchanges: they asked for gold. The British banking system had to face the truth: it held insufficient gold to honour all the claims issued. In Great Britain, monetary collapse became imminent.

The situation was similar in North America. But it was exacerbated by the acceptance of shares on the stock market as collateral for loans. Through the provision of up to 90 per cent of the purchase price of shares in the form of loans, "bidding power" was provided which drove the share market higher and higher. At each higher level, lenders remained willing to advance 90 per cent. The value of shares soon became unsupportable. Yet "bidding power" continued to drive them higher. In due course even the most optimistic investor began to suspect that share prices had far exceeded their actual value, and would no longer invest. The market collapsed. The inflated value of collateral disappeared. Individuals and institutional borrowers were unable to sell their shares to cover loans. Lenders found much of their collateral valueless. Lending stockbrokers and their supporting banks began to fall like tenpins.

So, by the early 1930's, monetary collapse in Great Britain and the United States of America as imminent. The monetary authorities of both countries ought to have recognised misrepresentation as the cause of the impending collapse. They ought to have exposed if and thereby helped the system to heal. Instead, they reasoned that if individuals had been willing to accept paper claims at a given value on one day, they ought to be able to accept them at a similar value the following day. Confidence in the exchange value of the invalid claims had to be created. Both governments therefore chose to legitimise the claims. They made them the only legal medium of exchange. They cancelled the convertibility of these claims to gold by other than governments. They banned the use of gold itself as a medium of exchange.

Thus the prudent and the careful, who had chosen to hold gold rather than paper, paid the penalty and the careless and the fraudulent were let off the hook. Dishonesty was rewarded and integrity penalised.

Nevertheless, the validation of paper money might have solved the governments' monetary problems had action been taken to stop the continuing production of invalid receipts. But nothing was done to stop the banking practice of money-lending.

Therefore the issuance of invalid receipts continued. Now, however, it was worse: the deposit looked just like the paper receipt. Both were simply statements about pounds or dollars. It is and it remains difficult to differentiate between them. Today, in the absence of a clear understanding of how the mechanism actually works, the money supply appears to grow organically. Some would even say mysteriously. Yet there is nothing mysterious about it. By allowing the superimposition of the mechanism of money-lending onto the system for storing and distributing money we have both legitimised and institutionalised misrepresentation. Thereby we have allowed the emergence of a monetary and banking system which continues to debase the currency by its own natural action.

Paper Money

If we return to Mr Goldsmith and his new bank, and substitute a hundred dollars in paper money for the gold coin, the reason why there is no reality behind the current Western paper money system will unfold, and we shall discover why unless the system is altered, it will collapse. The same misrepresentation, two receipts against one deposit, will occur as it did when gold was the standard.

Accounting balance

Deposits:	$200	Cash:	$100
			$100
	$200		$200

Actual position

Receipts issued: $200

Stock in hand: $100

Yet it will not be as easy to see. Under the paper monetary system we are easily confused. The deposit looks just like the receipt. Each is usually merely a piece of paper with the number of units of money written on it. The logic of our former example, however, does also apply with paper money: although the bank's books will balance, the money supply will actually have doubled.

We are equally easily confused when trying to determine the value of current paper money. There is no real physically measurable substance behind a unit of paper money. Nor, when a loan is made, is there any real physically measurable substance or value behind any of the newly created units of money. Nor is there any real substance behind units which are deposited. They are not guaranteed to be exchangeable for any fixed amount of anything.

Their value comes from their being the only legal and valid medium of exchange. They are effectively a claim on everything and anything that is offered for sale in the market-place. The great difficulty is that both the amount of money and the volume and mix of the goods and services against which they can claim is continually changing. There is, therefore, little opportunity to measure accurately one against the other.

If the supply of units of money were fixed, when the demand for them increased, so too would their value; and as the demand for them decreased, their value would also decrease. There would be a minimum demand for units of money. It would represent the minimum volume of exchanges required for the population to survive. Thus, each unit of paper money would have a minimum exchange value.

Each would also have a maximum exchange value. It would represent the level of exchange value at which savers are motivated to withdraw their money from savings and use it to take advantage of its greater purchasing power. A withdrawal will then increase the volume of money used in exchanges, leading to a decrease in its exchange value.

Thus, it is possible to see how a fixed supply of paper money can lead to a range of exchange values between this minimum and maximum. In due course, the exchange value of a unit of money would begin to fluctuate more and more narrowly within this range, eventually leading to stability.

Unfortunately the money supply is not fixed. New units of money are virtually produced according to demand. Bankers create new units of money every time they create net new loans. They are in business exactly for this purpose. Their normal activity produces a continuing expansion of the money supply.

Governments are meant to control the money-creating activities of banks. Current controls, however, are not effective.

Legal Reserves

A system within which each bank must hold a specified portion of its deposits in investments known as Legal Reserves has been one of the principle mechanisms by which governments have tried to control the money supply. Legal Reserves are promissory notes issued by borrowers deemed least likely to default. They are therefore the most saleable or convertible into cash in the event of an emergency.

Under this system, a bank is theoretically limited to creating new units of money in an amount equal to that of its excess Legal Reserves. If, for instance, a bank had deposits of £50,000 and the reserve requirements were 20 per cent, it would be required to hold a minimum of £10,000 in recognised Legal Reserve instruments. Suppose the bank actually held £15,000 in such investments. It would have another £5,000 which it would be permitted to advance as loans to its customers, thereby creating new demand deposits.

When we look at the banking system as a whole, we immediately expose a major weakness. The system can actually create a much larger amount than the amount of excess reserves.

Suppose, for instance, that all of the excess reserves in the system were lodged in one bank, Barclays perhaps, and that each of the other banks was willing to receive new deposits and to issue new loans to the limit of its reserves. If Barclays had the £5,000 excess referred to above, and it created new units by lending them to me, and I then spent them on one purchase at Harrods, and Harrods deposited them at the Midland, then the Midland would have a new deposit of £5,000. The Midland would then be required to invest £1,000 or 20 per cent in Legal Reserves. It would then have £4,000 in excess reserves and could lend £4,000 to one of its clients. Its client could spend it similarly, and Lloyds might then receive £4,000, invest £800 in Legal Reserves, and lend £3,200 to one of its clients. This process could continue until approximately £25,000 had been created.

Thus while an individual bank is limited to the amount of its excess reserves, the system as a whole can produce new units in multiples of the total excess reserves within it.

Nor is this limitation absolute. If we look closely at Legal Reserves, they are themselves loans. For instance, many types of government securities, including Treasury Notes, are considered Legal Reserves, and, in some cases, so are bank-endorsed bills. Treasury notes are receipts issued by the government for money loaned to it. The government uses the borrowed money to meet it obligations. Bank-endorsed bills are also loans and are used by the borrower to meet his obligations. In both cases the money is immediately back in circulation. It will be re-deposited and then it will be available to be loaned again. Reserve instruments are not a protection against misrepresentation. They are actually themselves part of the very misrepresentation they profess to be controlling.

The only limitation imposed by the use of a Legal Reserve system is the borrowing requirements of the issuers of reserve instruments. Where their appetite is insatiable there is no limitation at all.

The production of money by Central Banks

Central banks produce new units of money via several mechanisms. The most obvious, of course, is the minting of new notes and coins. In most countries it is the Central Bank which is responsible for the mint. New notes and coins are produced either to replace old and worn or damaged ones, or to maintain sufficient cash in the system to service the needs of the daily transactions in the market-place. The need for cash varies from market-place to market-place. For instance, some companies still meet their payrolls using cash in small brown envelopes. Others use cheques. Some shops and businesses will accept credit cards or cheques. Others prefer cash. Each market will vary.

Nevertheless, in general, between 6 and 8 per cent of the total money supply needs to be in cash to keep the market-place functioning effectively. The rest can remain as entries on the books of banks, representing the deposits held in clients accounts. As the money-lending function of the banking system then expands the money supply, Central Banks are required to mint more and more cash just to keep this ratio.

Central Banks also put money into the market-place by what they call their "open market" activities. In these activities they buy and sell their government's debt instruments. If, for instance, a Central Bank buys government bonds or treasury certificates on the "open market", it is not providing cash to the government. It is providing cash to the former holder of the bond or certificate who will, presumably, then either spend it or invest it. Buying, thus, is intended to create more economic activity in the market-place.

Selling the certificates and bonds held, on the other hand, takes money from investors and, provided the Central Bank does not use that money for its own or government purposes, provided that the money simply remains unused within the Central Bank, the selling activity will reduce the amount of money available for investment and spending, thereby reducing the economic activity in the market-place. From the perspective of the money supply itself, when the Central Bank has to create new units of money to purchase bonds or certificates, the money supply will expand. Otherwise its activities will simply shift the location of existing units of money from one place to another, enticing them into savings (removing them from the market-place by a time factor), or causing them to be withdrawn from savings and spent or invested.

Foreign exchange transactions can also result in the production of new units of money by Central Banks. To see how this happens, suppose we were back in the days, when Central Banks could claim on each others' gold. Following the agreement between international Central Banks at Bretton Woods in the early 1940's individuals were no longer able to claim gold with their paper money or use gold as a medium of exchange, but governments could. Under the Bretton Woods Agreement each currency had a fixed exchange rate with the dollar and the dollar was guaranteed to be exchangeable for 1/35th of an ounce of gold; or $35 per ounce.

To see how this works, suppose that General Motors in America wanted to buy Land Rover in England, before 1971. General Motors would want to use dollars, the English owners of Land Rover would want to hold pounds. The English sellers, if they accepted dollars, would exchange them for pounds at their bank. If the bank had customers who wanted dollars, it would then exchange the dollars for pounds.

If the bank had no customers wanting dollars, it would look to the foreign exchange markets to exchange them for pounds. Failing that, it could exchange them for pounds at the Bank of England.

If the Bank of England had no pounds available to offer the commercial bank for the dollars, it would create them. The Bank of England would then take the dollars to New York to exchange them for gold. As a result it would receive an additional amount of gold into its reserves. So there would be no misrepresentation as a result of this transaction. In fact, the real money supply (the amount of gold itself) would have increased, decreasing the gap between the amount of gold required to satisfy all claims and the amount of gold actually held.

The position in America would be quite different. Once the dollars were returned to New York, the number of dollars in the American market-place would have returned to its previous level, but the amount of gold against which the dollars had been issued would have decreased by the amount given to the Bank of England in exchange for the returned dollars. So, in America, the gap between the amount of gold required to settle all claims and that actually available would have increased. Had General Motors borrowed the money at its bank, there would have been a double dose of the increase. New dollars would have been produced against existing levels of gold, and existing levels of gold would have been reduced by the amount transferred to the Bank of England.

The increase or decrease in the size of the gap occasioned by this transaction would be unlikely to have affected the exchange value of gold in either country. In each, the level of misrepresentation would already have been sufficiently vast to have pushed the exchange rate of gold to its minimum level.

So long as the exchange rate of gold itself did not change, and so long as both dollars and pounds were considered as valid claims against gold, then the domestic exchange value of dollars and pounds in their respective markets would also be unlikely to change. Therefore, under the gold system, or the dollar/gold system (following the Bretton Woods Agreement), prices would not have increased or decreased as a result of these foreign exchange transactions. Only the size of the respective gaps would have changed.

When President Nixon closed the gold window in 1971 a new era of the paper monetary system began. The importance of this change has not yet been widely recognised. Dollars can no longer be exchanged for a fixed amount of gold. Other currencies can no longer be exchanged for a fixed number of dollars. Each country's banking system will debase its currency at a different rate. There can be no fixed relationships. The floor beneath the value of the paper money has been removed. The value of each unit can now plumb untold depths.

The same transaction under the paper money system since 1971 will produce very different results in each country. As units of paper money are no longer freely exchangeable for gold by the issuer, the dollars cannot now be returned to America to be exchanged for gold. Instead they will be held by the Bank of England as reserves.

These dollars will be held either physically outside the United States, or on deposit with the Federal Reserve Bank in New York. They will be deposits set aside as a store of value for future use by the depositor. They will no longer be part of the US domestic money supply, but they will be part of the total US money supply. Being removed from their domestic market-place by a geographical factor, they will no longer have a direct affect on domestic US prices. But they will exist.

Their position will not be dissimilar to that of units of money removed from their domestic market-place by a time factor. A five-year deposit, for example, will play little part in the domestic market-place during its five-year term. The existence of such units of money is often effectively forgotten, only to become obvious when they mature and are redeposited as demand deposits. If inflation becomes so high that investors are unwilling to renew time deposits and will only redeposit funds as demand deposits, the money supply appears to increase dramatically. The apparent increase is false: money which had been removed by a time factor simply returns.

Similarly when units of money which have been removed from the market-place by a geographical factor return, the domestic money supply increases. But until they do return, the transaction between General Motors and the English sellers will have diminished the American money supply and reduced the amount of money available for exchanges unless, of course, the purchase was financed by a loan from General Motors' American bank.

If the purchase was financed by a loan, the new money created will have been exported. Previously existing units will not have been exported and thus the domestic money supply in the United States will remain unchanged.

In the meantime, back in England, the Bank of England will also have produced new units of money. They will have issued new pounds to exchange for the dollars received. So the British money supply will have increased.

Following Richard Nixon's decision to close the "gold window", the Bank of England is obliged to hold the dollars so acquired as reserves until market conditions change and they are needed to exchange for pounds. When they are exchanged for pounds, the pounds received in the exchange will not be destroyed. They will be used in accordance with the domestic money requirements of the Bank of England, and will remain a part of the British money supply. So the reduction in Bank of England reserves will not bring with it a commensurate reduction in the British money supply to compensate for the earlier production. The inflation produced by the foreign exchange transaction will remain in the British market-place.

When the dollars are returned to their domestic market-place, the American domestic money supply will increase and, where the transaction was financed by a loan, the inflation produced by the transaction will reach its ultimate objective: its own domestic market-place. In due course, all national currencies must return to their own domestic market-places. So the existing Eurodollar "mountain" can be seen as a continuing threat to the domestic exchange value of the dollar.

On the other hand, if market conditions were such that the dollars were required to finance a purchase in some other country, then those dollars would enter the Central Bank reserves of that other country. The money supply of the receiving country would then increase, and the inflationary effects of the transaction would be felt in yet another market-place.

Under the new paper money system, units of money removed from their domestic market-place can move from nation to nation, increasing each country's money supply en route, and leaving a continuous swell of inflation in their wake.

There are two primary dangers in this process. The one which we have already observed is the importation of inflation by the receiving nation. This can often be signalled when the reserves of a Central Bank increase. If these increases are due to the accumulation of foreign paper money, they might reflect foreign investment in the domestic market-place. If that is the case the domestic money supply will have increased proportionately, and it follows that the domestic purchasing power of that currency will, in due course, decrease.

The other, which is potentially more dangerous, is the ability of international banks and the international divisions of multinational banks to expand any nation's money supply. Consider, for example, Eurodollars: they are accepted as deposits and loaned with regularity by international bankers. These deposits and loans are unsupervised by any monetary authority. In this wider market-place there is no international Central Bank. So there is no lender of last resort, and no restrictions on the expansionary money-lending activities of these banks. The only practical limitation upon the productive capacity of these lending institutions are the willingness of borrowers to borrow, the credit worthiness of borrowers, and the prudence of international bankers.

Nor does the Exchange Rate Mechanism (ERM) stop inflation. It indexes a basket of individual currencies. Each individual currency will be being debased by its own banking system. Each will have no floor: have no level of depreciation beyond which it cannot go. The rate and extent to which each will be debased must, therefore, be different. The most that can be said for the ERM is that it is meant to synchronise the rate of debasement. It cannot stop it.

Imprudent behaviour

If history is an accurate guide to the future, we can confidently expect to see the number of claims, receipts or units of money in the world expand to a point of imprudence. From an historic perspective, first individual banks expanded their receipts and claims to the point of imprudence. Bank failures were experienced and the term bankruptcy was coined. Central Banks were then established as lenders of last resort to bailout individual banks which had reached their point of imprudence. The effect was, by giving them a safety net, to license all commercial banks to expand their operations to their individual points of imprudence. Central

Banks then allowed their national money supply to be expanded in multiples, until the international banking and monetary system as a whole reached its point of imprudence. This brought the collapse of the gold standard system.

It follows logically that the international banking community will now expand the world's paper money supply to its point of imprudence. Thus we must each ask ourselves some serious questions:

Will the entire system then collapse, destroying the savings and liquid assets of everyone, including our own?

Will the system's survival instinct produce yet another palliative which allows some parts of the banking system to survive and continue their current imprudent and destructive practises, while the remainder fails?

Will our savings and liquid assets be in the part that survives or the part that fails?

Would we not be wiser to take action now to correct the system and thus avoid the risk?

SPEECH MADE TO THE HOUSE OF LORDS, FEBRUARY 5th 2009

The Earl of Caithness, Malcolm Ian Sinclair (Conservative)

Editor's note: The following speech neatly encapsulates the faults in the banking system identified in the previous article, in the context of the most recent financial crisis

My Lords, the Banking Bill which we are currently discussing in the House is very complex and detailed, but it does nothing to resolve the current banking crisis, which lies at the heart of our economic problems. The noble Lord, Lord Peston, has just said that it is the fault of the bankers. I agree with him up to a point, but would go further and say that the fault that really needs correcting is our whole banking system. I am therefore grateful to the noble Lord, Lord Eatwell, for bringing forward this debate.

The Banking Bill fails to address the fault which has led to every major banking and currency crisis during the past 200 years, including this one. It merely, lazily and weakly, papers over the cracks. Like Lilliputians, we are trying to tie down Gulliver with ever more strands of rope. It did not work then; it has not worked since 1811; and it will not work now.

In March 1997, I warned in this House that our failure then to address the banking system would lead to greater hardship. I said:

"The cycle will continue, but the next time, as before, we will all start deeper in debt and with a burden harder to carry".—[Hansard, 5/3/97; col. 1871.]

We did not act then in the good times. However, I am reminded of Milton Friedman's observation that it takes a crisis for real change to occur. So what better time than now?

By January last year, I could see that the imprudence of bankers had exceeded even my worst fears and I introduced the Safety Deposit Current Accounts Bill to try to defuse the explosion that I could see coming. During the Second Reading debate in April, I asked under which Act of Parliament the current banking system had been established. I got no reply from the noble Lord, Lord Davies of Oldham, whom I am glad to see in his place. I asked again in November, in the debate on the Queen's Speech. Again, there was no reply. I understand that no Act has been passed by Parliament. The current crisis, like previous ones, emanated from a base of judicial decisions. Prior to 1811, title to the money in depositors' accounts belonged to the depositor. However, in that year, decisions in Carr v Carr and, in 1848, Foley v Hill gave legal status to the banking practice of removing depositors' money from their accounts and lending it to others. Since then, title to depositors' money has transferred from the depositor to the bank at the moment when the deposit is made.

Bankers have always seen it as their job to invest as much of their depositors' money as they prudently can, in order to earn income for themselves while, at the same time, maintaining sufficient cash flow to be able to honour depositors' cheques when presented and to meet withdrawals when demanded. If new deposits fail to materialise in sufficient strength or if borrowers fail to repay on time or at all, banks need to be rescued or they will fail. Historically, bank failures then led to a demand for central banks to act as lenders of last resort to save imprudent bankers who got caught short.

These judicial decisions meant that, from then until now, money deposited belonged to the bank and not the depositor, thereby allowing bankers to use customers' deposits as they saw fit, always provided that they could manage cash flow so as to meet depositors' requirements. In good times, that enabled them to take greater risks. Then, with the advent of central banks as lenders of last resort, the bankers soon learned they could take even greater risks with virtual impunity. When their lending became too aggressive and their reserves and deposit receipts were less than required to meet cash flow, they began to lend to each other. Banks with excess reserves would lend on the overnight market to those with a shortfall. With all these supposed safety mechanisms to protect them, bankers came to believe they could become even more aggressive in their lending, enabling them to make increased profits for themselves.

The provision of these safety mechanisms had, in some cases, merely encouraged them to take excessive risks. Further, these two judicial decisions overlooked or failed to consider the fact that when banks lend depositors' funds, more than one receipt for the same deposit is issued. This was not done intentionally by individual banks or it would immediately have been seen as fraudulent. Rather, it was done by the system as a whole. This process continued to the present. It is as a result that our UK money supply has grown from £31 billion in 1971, when President Nixon closed the gold window, to in excess of £1,700 billion today. Let us consider the implications of those last two figures. They mean that every year since 1971 the banking system has created, on average, for its own use, in excess of £44 billion. That is more per year than the entire money supply which had, until 1971, sustained our economy since recorded history and through two world wars. Is it any wonder that we have suffered such serious inflation over that period? It is clear that the normal, everyday onward lending of depositors' funds by retail banks has been the principal producer of inflation.

When paper money was backed by gold, this same production of new receipts by the banking system increased the number of claims for the gold held in reserve without in any way increasing the amount of gold available to meet them. Therefore, the amount of gold available for each receipt became smaller and the value of paper money decreased. The normal, everyday banking practice of onward lending of depositors' funds led to such a continued increase in the number of claims for the gold available that it caused a series of revaluations of paper money with respect to the amount of gold each could claim. The rates of increase varied from country to country, creating complexity in foreign exchange markets and leading to a series of international agreements to try to determine the correct relationship between various national currencies and gold. The last of these was the Bretton Woods agreement in 1944. It was breached in 1971, when the huge increase in the number of dollars created since 1944 forced President Nixon to close the gold window.

The same banking mechanism, which destroyed the gold standard, is now destroying the central banking system. Central banks can no longer cope. The Treasury and the taxpayer have now to try to pick up the pieces. In fact, the failures are so serious and banks have been so imprudent that they are now unwilling to lend to each other and Governments had to ask to kick-start inter-banking lending. In Davos recently, the world looked at the imperilled state of the western monetary system with shock, and there is so little faith in paper money that cries are heard for a new Bretton Woods. All that has occurred because of the failure of Governments, economists, the press and the public to recognise the faults in the banking system that were given legitimacy by those early judicial decisions.

Even today, the Government are striving to save this discredited system with still more legislation that attempts to control the degree to which this fraudulent but legal mechanism can continue to operate. Why are we trying to save a system that, since 1811, has overcome every attempt to harness it? Now is an excellent time to revisit the question of the banking system. We should consider in detail a system to correct the faults that I have identified by creating accounts that do not transfer title to depositors' money from depositors to the banks. Banks must not be allowed to continue to lend depositors' money without the consent of the depositor. This will immediately stop the issuance of two receipts against the same money. Depositors would have to pay for the storage and distribution of their money in accounts and banks would have to compete and earn their income through storage and distribution charges.

For those who wish to earn an income with their money and who wish banks to invest their savings for them, savings accounts are available. With those actions we can completely remove the duplication of receipts from the banking system and stabilise the money supply. Banks will no longer be able to lend depositors' funds. Depositors' funds will then be safe. There will be no further need for lenders of last resort. Taxpayers will no longer be required to bail out future bank failures and inflation can be halted in its tracks. Can it happen? Yes. Will it happen? That depends on the Government's response. My noble friend Lord Eatwell said, when he opened the debate, that we cannot return to the norm. We will, however, unless the Government grasp the nettle and cease throwing taxpayers' money at a faulty system and stop trying to control the uncontrollable. There can be no better time to act than now.

GUANTANAMO IN A LEGAL CONTEXT

By Anthony Davies, LL.B, LL.M

Editor's note: In the following paper, Anthony Davies highlights the legal decisions which paved the way for the detainees of Guantanamo Bay to regain legal rights and for the treatment to be more closely monitored and indeed more morally acceptable

Introduction

The debate revolving around the legality of the US run detention camp in Cuba called Guantanamo Bay has, since its establishment been a highly contested one especially within the circles of both International and Human Rights lawyers. The detention facility is within territory controlled by the United States, which have an indefinite lease on the land from Cuba. Held there are persons believed terrorists, who have been incarcerated by the United States government for the object of keeping such out of mainstream society. Most are believed to be held through their connection with Al-Qaeda whilst the current Bush Administration conducts their 'war on terror'.

The object of this paper will take several roles; firstly I believe it is pertinent that we attempt to establish how the detainees are treated within the camp, including issues surrounding interrogation techniques adopted solely for these detainees, and also the issue of the denial to the prisoners a fair trial or even to know the reason for their detention.

Secondly a substantial look into what individuals and International bodies trying to help the detainees have already accomplished or are trying to accomplish will be investigated, whilst comparing and contrasting the efforts made by them and to those of the efforts which the Presidential Administration has done in response. Plus a brief insight into how the English Courts have ruled on the British citizens that are held. Thirdly an all important delve into the unknown of what the future will/should hold and just how this may be done. Here we will look at relatively low powered NGO's to the immense potential power of the United Nations, including their efforts so far, there current positioning and just what is available for continued efforts.

Detainee Treatment at Guantanamo

At present the persons detained at Guantanamo Bay are held in 'Camp Delta' which was created due to the fact after the terrorist attacks on the US of September 11th 2001 the United States required more space than the then 'Camp X-ray' could hold. Reports from released prisoners and many FBI agents bring to light the appalling conditions in which prisoners are held and treated within the Cuban facility. Both have complained especially of how prisoners are treated by way of interrogation, with particular reference to the Third Geneva Convention, Article 3 which makes reference to:

> '. . .each Party to the conflict shall be bound to apply, as a minimum, the following provisions: . . .Persons taking no active part in the hostilities, including members of armed forces who have...[been detained].
> . .shall in all circumstances be treated humanely, without any adverse distinction founded on race, colour, religion or faith, sex, birth or wealth, or any other similar criteria. To this end the following acts are and shall remain prohibited at any time and in any place whatsoever with respect to the above-mentioned persons: . . . cruel treatment and torture . . . outrages upon personal dignity, in particular, humiliating and degrading treatment . . . the passing of sentences . . . without

previous judgment pronounced by a regularly constituted court affording all the judicial guarantees which are recognized as indispensable by civilized peoples.'[1]

Which the United States was a signatory to in 1949. However the Bush Administration does not recognise the detainees at Guantanamo Bay as POW's (prisoners of war) and therefore does not regard them as having the rights contained within the Convention. According to the US, Article 4 protecting civilians in much the same way as Article 3 can also not apply, with the detainees being labelled by them as 'enemy combatants'. Which invented by the US has very little meaning with the rest of the world. It is also worth noting that it is especially difficult to evaluate the term 'enemy combatant' in regards to existing Conventions and Treaties, since currently no reference can be found.

Interrogation

Since the right to POW status does not apply to the detainees held in Guantanamo Bay the US sanctioned the allowance of interrogation techniques to be used on the prisoners which contravene all current allowance through International customary law and in particular the Geneva Convention (albeit not recognised as afforded to the Guantanamo detainees). A memo signed by the then Secretary of Defence for the US, Donald Rumsfeld allowed for techniques far and beyond normal interrogation guidelines, there were to be three successive stages adopted for escalation depending on the 'compliance' of the detainee, included in this memo were the allowance of:

- 'The use of stress positions (like standing), for a maximum of four hours.
- Use of the isolation facility for up to 30 days.
- The use of 28 hour interrogations.
- Using detainees individual phobias . . . to induce stress.
- The use of scenarios designed to convince the detainee that death or severely painful consequences are imminent for him and/or his family.

- Use of a wet towel and dripping water to induce the misperception of suffocation.'[2]

Mr Rumsfeld when signing to agree to the measures only made comment that instead of four hour stress positions he had no objection to doubling that to eight hours, noting 'However, I stand for 8–10 hours a day. Why is standing limited to 4 hours?'[3] The memo is one of the most astonishing documents I have read to date, with the blatant sanctioning of torture, or borderline torture being endorsed by a person employed in a highly authoritative position within the executive branch of Government. No regard has been made in keeping to basic humane treatment towards persons within your control, and is a violation of more international agreement than for the purpose of this paper one will even attempt to list. Although extremely severe are the interrogation techniques that are used, a more fundamental right is not afforded to the prisoners held by the US at Guantanamo Bay. The basic rule introduced by the Magna Carta[4] of *habeas corpus*.

Habeas Corpus

This basic right of *habeas corpus* is:

> 'a prerogative writ used to challenge the validity of a person's detention . . . If on an application for the writ the Court of judge is satisfied that the detention is prima facie unlawful, the custodian is ordered to appear and justify it, failing which release is ordered.'[5]

Since America's beginning as a sovereign State the writ of *habeas corpus* has always existed. Most nations including the US remain to have the option to revoke the use of such a writ during times of 'national security', but once order is resumed so must the availability to invoke the writ. However the detainees currently held at 'Camp Delta' are not entitled by the US Government to apply for judicial review on the validity of their detention as they are 'enemy combatants', and up till recently not viewed as being held on US soil. In short denying the allowance of one of the world's oldest and most respected human right to detainees. The overwhelming right to an individual to know the reason to his detention and be adjudicated upon charges brought before him in a sanctioned court has been the most legally contested aspect of the treatment to detainees at Guantanamo Bay. The indefinite detention of any person by a State or even an individual touches upon too long of a fundamental right for it to be overlooked, and therefore many cases have arisen in response to this blatant violation by the US Government.

Intervention to date

Human Rights and International lawyers, including authoritative bodies have battled in relative vain to attempt for the current (and former) detainees at Guantanamo to be given the basic rights for which all of human kind should be allowed. However there has been no let up to the continuation of defence for the prisoners currently held under the US's 'war on terror.' In recent years documentation of treatment and individual accounts of Guantanamo Bay's conduct have astonished even the hardiest of readers. But progress even if rather slow to start with is thankfully gathering great momentum, the first effort to resolve issues of Guantanamo Bay came by way of the case *Rasul v Bush*[6].

Within the United States

Rasul v Bush

The Supreme Court in this first case ruled in favour of the detainees in regards to challenging the legality of their imprisonment on grounds of *habeas corpus*. Justice Kennedy says on the grounds of Guantanamo Bay being US territory:

> 'In a formal sense, the United States leases the Bay; the 1903 lease agreement states that Cuba retains "ultimate sovereignty" over it. Lease of Lands for Coaling and Naval Stations, Feb. 23, 1903, U. S.-Cuba, Art. III, T. S. No. 418. At the same time, this lease is no ordinary lease. Its term is indefinite and

at the discretion of the United States. What matters is the unchallenged and indefinite control that the United States has long exercised over Guantanamo Bay. From a practical perspective, the indefinite lease of Guantanamo Bay has produced a place that belongs to the United States, extending the "implied protection" of the United States to it.'[7]

And goes on later to say:

'In light of the status of Guantanamo Bay and the in-definite pretrial detention of the detainees, I would hold that federal-court jurisdiction is permitted in these cases. This approach would avoid creating automatic statutory authority to adjudicate the claims of persons located out-side the United States. . .'[8]

This was an early and potentially land breaking victory for the detainees, which resulted in the Centre for Constitutional Rights (CCR) lodging over 500 applications for *habeas corpus* in a lawsuit called *John Does Nos. 1-570 v Bush*[9] for the remaining detainees yet to challenge the legality of their detention. However, the ability for such an application on ground of *habeas corpus* was short lived, with the introduction of the 'Graham-Levin' legislative amendment. This was later approved by President Bush and became part of the Detainee Treatment Act 2005, even though there was great pressure from the CCR and various human rights organisations. The most important section of that Act reads:

'. . . no court, justice, or judge shall have jurisdiction to hear or consider . . . an application for a writ of habeas corpus filed by or on behalf of an alien detained by the Department of Defense at Guantanamo Bay, Cuba; or . . . any other action against the United States or its agents relating to any aspect of the detention by the Department of Defense of an alien at Guantanamo Bay, Cuba. . .'[10]

Thus retaining all ability to define the detainees held at Guantanamo within the executive branch of the United States, resulting in no availability to the remaining prisoners to challenge their right to unlawful detention outside of prescribed Courts within the military, known as Combatant Status Review Tribunals (CSRT). Only, within the trial at a CSRT the detainee is not permitted to have counsel or present witnesses, they also have no knowledge of their charge and cannot even present evidence in their defence. Not to be deterred by the new Act another detainee of Guantanamo Bay, Salim Ahmed Hamdan brought a case under the writ of *habeas corpus* in 2006.

Hamdan v Rumsfeld

Salim was purchased by the United States from his captures in Afghanistan and sent to Guantanamo Bay. He was later charged with conspiracy to commit terrorism in July 2004, with a trial to be held at Guantanamo by a military commission. Halim refused to recognise the military commission's validity to try his case as it lacked the protections that are required by the Geneva Conventions and the United States Uniform Code of Military Justice (UCMJ). The Supreme Court gave its decision on *Hamdan v Rumsfeld*[11] on the 29th June 2006. Justice Stevens on giving the opinion of the court said on the issue of the Detainee Treatment Act 2005:

> '. . . the DTA cannot be read to authorize this commission. Although the DTA. . . was enacted after the President had convened Hamdan's commission, it contains no language authorizing that tribunal or any other at Guantanamo Bay. The DTA obviously "recognize[s]" the existence of the Guantanamo Bay commissions in the weakest sense. . .because it references some of the military orders governing them and creates limited judicial review of their "final decision[s]. . . But the statute also pointedly reserves judgment on whether "the Constitution and laws of the United States are applicable" in reviewing such decisions and whether, if they are, the "standards and procedures" used to try Hamdan and other detainees actually violate the "Constitution and laws."'[12]

The supreme court further held that the commission set up at Guantanamo Bay was insufficient at providing basic protection that are required by both the UCMJ and the Geneva Conventions, inadequacies of the commission were noted in several aspects, namely:

- '• The defendant and the defendant's attorney can be forbidden to view certain evidence used against the defendant, and the defendant's attorney can be forbidden to discuss certain evidence with the defendant;
- • Evidence judged to have any probative value may be admitted, including hearsay, unsworn live testimony, and statements gathered through torture; and
- • Appeals are not heard by courts, but only within the Executive Branch.'[13]

The Court held that the commission grossly contravened in this respect, Common Article 3 of the Geneva Conventions, which strictly disallows 'the passing of sentences and the carrying out of executions without previous judgment pronounced by a regularly constituted court, affording all the judicial guarantees which are recognized as indispensable by civilized peoples'. Even with a second damming decision from the Supreme Court the Executive were in no way despondent and within only four months after the hearing, returned with the enactment of the Military Commission Act 2006.

This right crushing document provided a multitude of unbelievable albeit interesting points on the treatment of detainees at Guantanamo Bay, initially at section 3, sub section 1 on General Provisions, parts (f) and (g) of 948b state:

'. . .A military commission established under this chapter is a regularly constituted court, affording all the necessary 'judicial guarantees which are recognized as indispensable by civilized peoples' for purposes of common Article 3 of the Geneva Conventions. . .No alien unlawful enemy combatant subject to trial by military commission under this chapter may invoke the Geneva Conventions as a source of rights.'

In quick succession noting that the Commissions to be convened are legal according to common Article 3, however the detainees have no right to challenge their defence on grounds contained within the same Convention. Then under section 7 relating to *Habeas Corpus Matters* the legislation, not only denies the right to challenge illegal detention, but also the physical treatment of the detainees, it reads:

> '. . .No court, justice, or judge shall have jurisdiction to hear or consider an application for a writ of habeas corpus filed by or on behalf of an alien detained by the United States who has been determined by the United States to have been properly detained as an enemy combatant or is awaiting such determination. . .no court, justice, or judge shall have jurisdiction to hear or consider any other action against the United States or its agents relating to any aspect of the detention, transfer, treatment, trial, or conditions of confinement of an alien who is or was detained by the United States and has been determined by the United States to have been properly detained as an enemy combatant or is awaiting such determination.'

Now we can see that even though lawyers and organisations have been attempting to gain rights for the detainees held at Guantanamo which should be afforded to all citizens on a global scale, let alone people under the control of one of the largest democratic States internationally. There plights have been nothing short of futile faced with the awesome power exerted by the current US Administration to enact into law the removal of any rights that their own Supreme Court has found in favour of. A steady pattern can clearly be seen from the cases and then legislation discussed above, and now recently in 2008 once again the table has turned in favour of the detainees by way of *Boumediene v Bush.*[14]

Boumediene v Bush

Decided by the Supreme Court on the 12 June 2008 by a majority of 5 to 4, this most recent of decisions appears to have been the final 'nail in the coffin' for the Bush Government in their attempt to suppress the rights of detainees they hold without charge in Cuba on their ‚war on terror’. Although the margin of defeat for Bush is by a single judge, the decision stands as a great triumph for the current prisoners. And not only have jubilations been felt by the detainees, around the globe a strong sense of that feeling is held by many, from campaigners appealing for such a result for many years to those whom just feel that the terrible atrocities that have been stricken upon the uncharged, in humanely kept detainees seems eventually to have an ending well within sight.

Justice Kennedy giving the majority opinion in *Boumediene v Bush* offered a lengthy review of the history of *habeas corpus* and whether its reach extended beyond U.S. borders. Anticipating that some might think the history lesson was unnecessary, Kennedy wrote, ‘Remote in time it may be; irrelevant to the present it is not’, summing up rather beautifully *habeas corpus* in one sentence. He continued, ‘Security depends upon a sophisticated intelligence apparatus and the ability of our Armed Forces to act and to interdict. There are further considerations, however. Security subsists, too, in fidelity to freedom’s first principles.’

Addressing concerns about national security, Kennedy said, ‘Liberty and security can be reconciled; and in our system they are reconciled within the framework of the law. The Framers decided that habeas corpus, a right of first importance, must be a part of that framework, a part of that law’, concluding that the administration had yet again gone too far in restricting civil liberties, even in wartime. He made caution to saying that the ruling does not necessarily mean that the detainees will be freed, only more rights must be observed.

The Court continued to go even further, ruling as well on the merits of whether the alternative method devised by Congress in the Detainee Treatment Act to deal with detainee appeals was sufficient of even legal. Noting that some detainees have been held for six years, the majority agreed that it should not bounce that issue back to lower courts. Because of procedural inadequacies, the Court ruled that the alternate review process created by Congress amounts to ‘an unconstitutional suspension of the writ' of habeas corpus. 'The costs of delay can no longer be borne by those who are held in custody. The detainees in these cases are entitled to a prompt habeas corpus hearing.' With a 5 to 4 majority ruling there were obviously opposing feelings.

One of the dissenting judge's, Justice Antonin Scalia gave the opinion that due to the outcome of the decision there will now exist '. . . the impossible task of proving to a civilian court, under whatever standards the Court devises in the future, that evidence supports the confinement of each and every enemy prisoner', ending with 'The nation will regret what the Court has done today.'

I believe that one can only agree with the outcome decided upon by the majority in this instance, and with special regards to the comments of Justice Scalia find his an unbelievable analysis to reasoning for the allowance to detain people indefinitely without charge. There can be numerous cases in which proving guilt in a civilian court is a difficult task; however the only way to assure any justice is to do just that. As yet no challenge to the decision has been made by the Bush Administration, and considering the current climate in the US towards President Bush and his soon to be handover of Presidency, it would seem highly unlikely that any new legislation will be drafted to attempt to overhaul this decision. Before we move on to take a look into how the international system as a whole has dealt with, and what they can do in time to overcome the issue of detainees at Guantanamo, I believe it important to look at how the English Courts have dealt with cases involving prisoners at the camp.

The United Kingdom's View

R (on the application of Abbasi) v Secretary of State for Foreign and Commonwealth Affairs

The first case heard within an English Court was that of Feroz Abbasi, in *R. (on the application of Abbasi) v Secretary of State for Foreign and Commonwealth Affairs.*[15] Mr Abbasi was a British National held at the American's Cuban facility. He wished for the English Courts to rule in favour to his plea that Britain owed him a public law duty, to take all reasonable steps to secure his release from Guantanamo Bay given that he was subject to a violation by the United States of one, of what he believed to be his fundamental human rights, namely *habeas corpus*. Lord Phillips gave the judgement for the court; dismissing Mr Abbassi's case he made the following comments:

'It is clear that international law has not yet recognised that a State is under a duty to intervene by diplomatic or other means to protect a citizen who is suffering or threatened with injury in a foreign State. . .the Foreign and Commonwealth Office have considered Mr Abbasi's request for assistance. He has also disclosed that the British detainees are the subject of discussions between this country and the United States both at Secretary of State and lower official levels. . .if the Foreign and Commonwealth Office were to make any statement as to its view of the legality of the detention of the British prisoners, or any statement as to the nature of discussions held with United States officials, this might well undermine those discussions. . .we do not consider that the **European Convention on Human Rights and the Human Rights Act [1998]** afford any support to the contention that the Foreign Secretary owes Mr Abbasi a duty to exercise diplomacy on his behalf.'

Therefore the English Court made it clear back in 2002 in this case that it was not within their jurisdiction to hear cases on such merits, leaving and decisions that would be made in respect of British Nationals to the sole discretion of the executive department, and in particular to that of the Secretary of State. Even so, in 2006 a case was brought before the English Courts in respect to non-British Nationals whom had however been granted British residency through asylum.

R (on the application of Al-Rawi) v Secretary of State for Foreign and Commonwealth Affairs

The case of *R (on the application of Al-Rawi) v Secretary of State for Foreign and Commonwealth Affairs*[16] unsurprisingly upheld the decision held in Mr Abbasi's case, in summary the court held on their applications that:

The detainees had been treated differently from British nationals not because of their nationality, but because they were not entitled to diplomatic protection, while British nationals were. Their circumstances were not the same as those of British nationals, so there was no violation of s.1(1)(a) of the 1976 Race Relations Act

For the same reason, the appellant family members could not make a case of discrimination. Since the secretary of state had not discriminated against the detainees, neither the detainees nor their families could complain that the secretary of state had failed to treat like cases alike. The only legitimate expectation the detainees had was that the secretary of state would consider a British national's request that representations be made on his behalf. In any event it was clear that the secretary of state had considered the detainees' requests.

The source of the family members' grievance was the actions of the US. The 1998 Human Rights Act contained no requirement that a signatory state should take up the complaints of any individual within its territory in relation to acts of another sovereign state

The detainees could not (as they wished to) rely on the International Law Commission's draft Articles on Diplomatic Protection, which proposed that a state may exercise diplomatic protection in respect of refugees or stateless persons. The Articles were not relevant as they could not be treated as existing law. Furthermore, they did not impact on the secretary of state's primary factual position, which was that to make representations on behalf of the detainees would be ineffective and counter-productive.

As we can clearly see from both above sited cases from English Courts that they have been more than a little reluctant in taking any purposeful action towards release of the British citizens held at Guantanamo. This I do not see as grave mistake by English Courts, they have simply upheld that in issues such as these their jurisdiction is more than a little limited, if any existence can be found at all. It quite rightly is in such cases an executive and diplomatic problem for the Government or indeed Parliament to resolve. To that end if executive intervention is a priority in the continuation of helping the remaining detainees in Guantanamo Bay then the United Kingdom cannot do it alone. There is now, more than ever, the need for increased international pressure on the United States to ensure the current situation is, as swiftly as possible and within common legal understanding finally resolved.

What is required of the international forum

The result of the *Boumediene v Bush* case has thankfully initiated a well overdue kick start to the recognition of the rights to which the detainees held at the camp in Guantanamo are entitled to. Now however the need to ensure that a high standard of pressure is put on the US to carry out lawful trials may have to become an international issue. There is far too much 'hear say' from different countries around the globe noting their disappointment in the way the United States has treated the detainees on their 'war on terror', condemnation as been heard since the opening of the facility at Cuba for long term un-tried prisoners, but so far no real heavy handedness has occurred. The only real pressure has come from the international human rights and humanitarian campaign groups such as the Red Cross.

NGO's

In particular the International Committee of the Red Cross (ICRC) has played a vital role for the protection of detainees held at Guantanamo Bay, they have as much as possible visited detainees there, with figures showing in their annual report of 2006 that they had visited 498 prisoners with a total of 407 of those being seen and monitored on an individual basis over a span of 20 visits.[17] Then in their 2007 report indicating that they had visited the same number of detainees, on the same number of visits, however only seeing 355 detainees individually.[18] Sadly the ICRC has been the only Non-Governmental Organisation (NGO) reported to have access within the confines of Guantanamo's perimeter fences to evaluate and talk to detainees, but what access they have been given, gave at least them an insight as to some of the issues to which we are now aware. Needles to say the ICRC are still committed to ensuring that the remaining prisoners held at Guantanamo are adorned with the correct amount of rights as international and human rights law allows them. NGO's cannot however be expected to do all the work in favour of the detainees, and since their powers are purely persuasive and non-existent of any real impact on the US as a whole, the requirement for higher powers within the world are required to add to their efforts.

The European Union

A good place to start would be that of Europe and the ever growing Union that is the spine of a very powerful set of nations, especially when pulled together as one. The only European stance has been taken by a writ submitted by 383 parliamentarians preceding the case of *Boumediene v Bush* in which they put forward mainly their views on the *habeas corpus* issues surrounding the detainees.[19] In their conclusion of this paper the 383 submitted:

> 'In this submission, [we] have showed a number of fundamental respects in which the CSRT process and insulating Petitioner' continued detention from *habeas* review or its equivalent departs from the fundamental rule of law and human dignity values embodied in treaties to which the United States is a party or a signatory, including the ICCPR, the ACHR and the Torture Convention. [We] are fully aware that the threat of terrorism is real. Governments around the world confront the dangers, and the hard choices posed by confronting those dangers, on an ongoing basis. The support for international law, human rights and the rule of law articulated in this brief comes, therefore, not from any underestimation of the terrorist threat, but rather from a keen appreciation of the extent to which those principles and values which most obviously distinguish us from those who target us with terror are endangered. To meet the danger the world needs not only military might, but renewed and sustained commitment to the rule of law and to fundamental

principles of human dignity and respect for human rights. In short, the world needs the United States to resume its role as a standard bearer for the principles of the rule of law and the protection of human rights and fundamental freedoms which are the shared heritage of a civilized world—and which are the heritage that together we seek to defend against the terrorist threat.'

Whether this played any sort of bearing on the judges decisions who adjudicated over the case of *Boumediene v Bush* we shall never know, it is just a shame that there was no direct action from the European Commission itself. Once again like the ICRC it has taken a group of people get together when their 'heart strings' are pulled just a little too much to actually make an impact on the atrocities that were occurring at Guantanamo. One hopes that now an official decision in *Boumediene v Bush* has been made the European Union may 'offer to lend support' to the American's in finally clearing up the issue of how to controllably deal with Guantanamo Bay. Even though the EU could lend great assistance and if required place some pressure on the US to clean up the Guantanamo detention centre, it would be far more beneficial for an international forum such as the UN to become deeply involved.

The United Nations

No doubt the largest source of power in the world is derived from the United Nations. There has certainly not been silence in the opinions from the UN on the treatment or indefinite detention of the detainees held. Since reports started to gather on the treatment of prisoners the UN has wholly condemned the facility. The most expressive arm of the UN being that of the Human Rights Council. It is great to see that the United Nations have praised so highly the decision by the Supreme Court in *Boumediene v Bush* and one only hopes that praise turns into a continuation of positive encouragement towards the end of Guantanamo, which I have no doubt it will. The only concern arises to a situation in which we are all too familiar with – that of the US Government somehow sidestepping the *Bourmediene* decision and carrying on as before the ruling.

If the US is to adopt this stance, it can only be said that intervention from the United Nations would prove to be very difficult. Since the United States holds the position of a permanent member on the Security Council, it also with that controls the ability to veto any conditions that are proposed to be issued on a Member State. Even with this power there is always a way in which 'deals' may be struck within the Security Council, and there is now, more than ever a need to apply pressure on the US to ensure that the current ruling of *Bourmediene* is not overruled by yet another executive decision.

A Combined Effort

All except the UN, no other single entity carries enough weight to ensure that America ensures for fair trials, and humane treatment for the remaining detainees held at Guantanamo. There needs to be an overwhelming bombardment from a multitude of organisations to pursue and ensure even the basic rights of the detainees still held by the United States are adhered to. Although this is difficult to implement, apart from the UN taking America head on itself, a necessity it is.

Conclusion

The analysis of Guantanamo Bay has been both an interesting and somewhat emotional journey. Even though so much of what has or is happening in the camp has been written by the press nothing prepares you for a deep evaluation of just how these actions of disregard to human treatment came into being.

We have documented many aspects of the physical and mental abuse that the detainees have had to endure during their 'stay' in Guantanamo, and seen how the US Government acted disgracefully in endorsing such approached to interrogation. Appalling too was the denial of the one basic right to any person in detention – that of the denial to file a writ of *habeas corpus*. Once again this was through the unethical actions of the US Government, classing the detainees as 'enemy combatants' and thus not affording them rights under their own constitution or even the Geneva Conventions, which apply at all times to all of humanity.

Initially in the US hope was gained by and for the detainees in the first ground breaking case of *Rasul v Bush,* gaining for the detainees a right to file for *habeas corpus* in civilian courts outside the military commission within the camp. Soon after, the United States removed this power by enacting the Detainee Treatment Act 2005, with its inclusion of the 'Graham-Levin' amendment. Next came the *Hamdan v Rumsfeld* case in 2006, with the Supreme Court once again reinstating the rights of the Guantanamo detainees, only for retaliation by the Bush Administration of the also in 2006 legislation of the Military Commission Act, once again crushing the rights to which the detainees were allowed. Thankfully however the current situation after the ruling in *Boumediene v Bush* the remaining detainees at Guantanamo are once again able to challenge their rights of indefinite detention without charge.

The English Courts made an interesting inclusion in the analysis, showing the view of what could be expressed as the probable view of any other jurisdiction opinions on the situation. As the Courts had (in their opinion) no right to hear cases with regard to how a foreign State deals with detainees under their control it remained a political issue for the executive to negotiate for any resolution if they saw themselves obliged to do so. However, there had been some intervention from one particular NGO.

The International Commission of the Red Cross played an important role in helping the detainees, not only on an individual basis but also as a negotiator for better rights for them with the US Government. But only the ICRC has played any sort of physical intervention towards the resolution of gaining rights for the detainees, with notice that important international 'power houses' such as the UN although condemning the actions of the United States have as yet made no formal requests for application to end the detainees treatment.

The current outlook for the remaining detainees seems to be positive, especially in regards to the Bush Administration not attempting to revoke the current decision of the Supreme Court by enacting more legislation. President Bush is extremely close to his end as the US's President and Commander-in-Chief, and although keen to keep the detainees indefinitely without charge will almost definitely not wish to 'waste' his final months in office trying to overturn the ruling. Whoever takes on the new role in the US, will have hopefully just a modicum of compassion regarding the detainees to whom he will take control over, allowing for the last Administrations enactments to cease to apply. If this turns out not to be the case, a certain intervention on an international scale will be required, and that would be most effective from the United Nations, anything short of this will only fuel the discontent that surrounds 'Camp Delta' and Guantanamo Bay.

9/11 AND THE NEW GLOBAL TERRORISM: CAN UNCONVENTIONAL ATTACKS BE EXPLAINED BY CONVENTIONAL THEORIES?

By Frederick Motson, LL.B, Barrister

Editor's note: This article was written for a conference in early 2007. However, it is the author's belief that the points raised remain relevant today.

Introduction

"One does not apply theory to history; rather one uses history to develop theory"

Arthur S. Stinchcombe, US Sociologist

At 08:46am on the 11th of September, 2001, the hijacked American Airlines Flight 11 was flown by Al-Qaeda operatives into the north tower of the World Trade Centre in New York. 17 minutes later, United Airlines Flight 175 was also purposefully crashed into the south tower. A third airliner was flown into the Pentagon. Between those on board these planes and a fourth hijacked plane which crashed in a field in New Jersey, those in the buildings hit and the rescue workers and volunteers who raced to the scene, the final death toll stood at 2,974[20]. Thousands more were injured. The attack was the most brutal, deadly and public terrorist incident on Western soil in history. It has led, directly or indirectly, to hundreds of thousands more deaths through the US response to the attacks, the so called "War on Terror". Today, multinational forces are still fighting a bitter war in Afghanistan, have not fully left Iraq and other countries which have supported terrorist groups, most notably Iran, are far from reconciled with the international community. If there is to be any resolution of the ideological, economic and historical clashes which have become the focus of international relations since 2001, the events of that day must be interpreted. International relations theorists have been quick to explain the attacks from almost every conceivable theoretical viewpoint. The aim of this paper is to examine and review the differing explanations offered by theorists from all of the 'main' schools of theory, including realists, liberals, structuralists and critical theorists, and also to investigate how far the relatively new approach of social constructivism can illuminate this area. How far do any of these theories explain why 9/11 occurred? How far do they agree or differ in attributing responsibility to different causes? And most importantly, can they offer any lessons for the future?

It ought to be noted at this point that while "9/11" has become a byword for terrorism, the ambit of this paper is wider than this single attack. However, the events of that September morning and the following bombings in Madrid[21] and London[22] heralded the rise to pre-eminence of a new form of terrorism – no longer focussed on "theatre"[23] but on inflicting maximum casualties; no longer spurred by understandable political goals but by religious fanaticism and hatred of an entire way of life; no longer occurring in unfamiliar third world nations but on the soil of the US and other Western powers; in London and Madrid no longer perpetuated solely by foreign nationals but by the nation in question's own citizens; and perhaps no longer explainable within existing IR frameworks.

Realism: A state-centric approach to a non-state phenomenon?

Realists have traditionally conceptualised international relations as the competition for power between sovereign states, dating back to the works of Thucydides[24]. Realists assert that the state is the overwhelmingly most important actor in world affairs because due to the anarchic nature of international relations, citizens' only hope of protection comes from a state powerful enough to deter others. This is a persuasive argument and the state would appear to be perhaps the most useful unit of analysis when measuring 'conventional' conflicts such as World War I. Yet the men who hijacked the airliners on September 11th were not 'soldiers'[25] and represented no particular state or alliance. Many were Saudi in origin, traditionally one of the US's closer allies in the Middle East. The problem for realists, and indeed for the US government, is how exactly to interpret an attack by a terrorist network which transcends national borders.

In the short-term, the US' answer was to invade Afghanistan. The ruling Taleban regime was seen as having organised and financed of 9/11, using so-called "state-sponsorship" of terrorism. This has been the position followed by classical realists at least since 9/11 – while most states linked to terrorism are not at war, underneath the surface the current global situation remains one in which states are competing for power – all that has changed is the methods they use to obtain it. In the words of President Bush, addressing Congress on the evening of the attacks, "Any nation that continues to harbour or support terrorism will be regarded, by the United States, as a hostile regime"[26]. These remarks were expanded upon by Henry Kissinger, one of the most (in)famous realist scholars as well as a former US Secretary of State, in a speech a month later[27]. Kissinger referred to the problems of "the shadowy nature of the challenge… [where terrorism] exists in many cells all over the world" but he again sees the phenomenon as rooted in, rather than transcending, sovereign states. "[Terrorism] cannot survive without some base…areas that provide organisation, recruitment, fund-raising and a sort of coherence" . In other words, just one month after the attacks, Kissinger was already raising the possibility of a longer list of terrorist supporting states than merely Afghanistan.

However, the realist perspective can also include the view that the 9/11 attacks merely gave George Bush the opportunity to invade various Middle Eastern countries which contained the resources, primarily oil, which America wishes to control. It should be noted that not only were Kissinger's remarks delivered in a speech rather than in a scholarly paper, but also that his close ties to successive administrations, including, it is alleged, with the current Bush presidency[28], may colour his views.

That is perhaps an argument more suited to political debate than international relations theory, however it can be said that whether one believes US intervention (or invasion) in other nations is benevolent or mercenary, the realist view of the state at the centre of IR is again relevant. Thus in one way, perhaps particularly appropriate for a school of thought that has always prided itself on its pragmatism, realism has avoided the problem of stateless terrorism because the dominant hegemon has done the same. Realism is not designed to answer for the ills within a society which drive some of its members to extremism and fanaticism and the vast majority of its proponents would admit as much. Combs believes this is why terrorism has become the natural successor to the Cold War as the major influence on foreign policy (in Western nations, at least) – "as states stepped back from open warfare, but left many national groups angry and determined to seek justice by violent means…terrorism continues to constitute a clear and present danger, a weapon that is evolving often faster than the world community's responses to it."[29]

One must also remember that classical realism is not the only strain of realist thought. Structural realists, in particular Kenneth Waltz, have become increasingly important in maintaining realist thought in a rapidly changing world system. Waltz argues[30] that while it is true that states function in a 'self-help' system, relying on their own power to deter others, this is not to be blamed simply on 'human nature' (the traditional position evident in such diverse thinkers as Machiavelli, Hobbes and Morgenthau[31]). Instead, it is the 'structure', or rather almost entire lack of such, in the world system, which causes states to act selfishly. Without any dominant sovereign body, co-operation is too dangerous to embark upon unless facing annihilation by a common enemy. Thus a balance of power based on military capability emerges even when states act without malevolence.

Considering that Waltz makes no attempt to change realism's reliance on states as the unit of analysis, how is this applicable to 9/11 and the 'War on Terror'? The essential idea to take from the work of the structural realists is that even when states do not act in a provocative manner, this can be precisely how their behaviour is viewed by potential enemies. As each side increasingly mistrusts the other, they build larger military capabilities in an attempt to deter war, yet of course this provokes the other into continuing the arms race. These so-called "security dilemmas" are, for neo-realists, the main explanation for wars, 'cold' or 'hot' which are actually harmful for both sides. Thus while the USA would argue that their interventions in the Middle East, almost unqualified support for Israel and mistrust of Islam are simply natural reactions to the repeated terrorist attacks they have suffered in recent history (such as the Beirut bombing in 1983), many Muslims who do not necessarily support Al-Qaeda or terrorism feel increasing sympathy for such extreme methods because of what they see as unbridled arrogance and interference by the West, particularly America and Britain. This leads to further atrocities on both sides. "Terrorist violence, has too often created a cycle of violence…Each violent act frequently causes equally violent reactions. When the violence is unselective, when innocent people are victimized, the reactive violence is also likely to break all the rules…and thus be terrorist"[32]. The cycle of the 9/11 attack, followed by the invasion of Iraq and the bombings in London on 7th July 2005 is a good example of how security dilemma theory can be applied to modern day ideological conflict, although it can be argued that such cycles begun decades or even centuries previously, from Cold War proxy wars to the Crusades. Note the testament of London bomber Mohammad Sidique Khan, who claimed "Your democratically elected governments continuously perpetrate atrocities against my people all over the world."[33]

Liberalism: Can economic theory apply to religious fervour?

At the most superficial level liberalism would seem better placed than realism to interpret terrorism and the behaviour of substate organisations such as Al-Qaeda. While liberals trace the roots of their philosophy back to ancient Greece, they are at heart most influenced by the individualism of Smith, Locke and Kant, among others. By examining international relations from the point of view of 'all' actors rather than simply states, liberals do not suffer the problem of being tied to a single unit of analysis. Yet it has been cogently argued that few liberals have looked outside of multinational corporations (MNCs) and nongovernmental organisations (NGOs) in their analysis, at least prior to September 11[34]. Keohane, in his response to the events of that day[34], expressly acknowledges this fact - "They ignore the impact of religion, despite the fact that world-shaking political movements have so often been fuelled by religious fervour" - yet then abdicates responsibility for correcting this omission, claiming "few insights into religious motivations". Of course whether the policy-makers and diplomats charged with winning the 'war on terror' have any clearer insights is highly debatable.

However, the fact remains that for a theory which is so bound up with the autonomy of the individual and prescriptive thinking, liberalism has significantly failed to address global terrorism. It is submitted that this may stem from the fact that 'individualism' as a concept in liberal thought is far removed from the motivations of individuals such as Osama Bin Laden. For liberals beginning with Adam Smith[35], the individual is always 'rational' – defined as always making choices which produce the greatest net benefit.

Whether this is a realistic view of human decision-making is a far too lengthy discussion for the present work, yet it can be said with some certainty that even assuming that rationality is ever present among individuals, the Western liberal assumption that rational choice as motivated by the pursuit of wealth can be very different to the goals that motivate decisions in the real world, particularly among those motivated by religion or nationalism. For a religious fanatic, committing a suicide attack may seem the most rational choice in a lifetime – yet it is difficult for those in 'post-religious' (mainly European) societies to understand motives such as killing innocents in order to reach paradise. This is more than a mere etymological argument and will be returned to later – suffice it to say at this point that the normative approach of liberalism can be exceptionally problematic when describing a conflict increasingly seen as a "clash of civilisations"[36].

Liberalism's overriding concern with economics can also be very misleading when considering issues such as terrorism. While certain conflicts generally portrayed as religious or ideological often include a sizeable economic causal element (most notably the Israeli-Palestinian dispute)[37], it is difficult to portray the attacks on September 11th as economically motivated. Liberals believe that co-operative economic interdependence provides a net benefit while war imposes costs on the majority, thus economic self-interest is one of the main reasons that peace is maintained, and the related model of 'democratic peace theory'[38] holds that this is why (arguably) liberal democracies are highly unlikely to go to war with another – the majority of voters will be personally adversely affected by the war, whichever nation 'wins'. The converse of this theory is that where the relationship is not balanced and one state is heavily dependant on another, mistrust and anger will arise and war may be the ultimate outcome. It could thus be argued that in many such nations the majority of citizens may believe that they receive negligible benefits from economic co-operation, thus war becomes less of an irrational option. It is indisputable that many in the Middle East feel exploited by the West, particularly in relation to oil.

Furthermore, one innovative use of the theory of "complex interdependence" is to use it to explain the inability of states to contain terrorism. Combs notes that even "enemies" such as Israel and Iran are willing to trade weapons if the price is right. She argues that "The economic ties forged by such transactions make it difficult for nations to take firm stands against terrorism or terrorist groups sponsored by the recipient nations. The stronger the economic linkage, the weaker is a government's response to restrict terrorism".[39] The vendor nation will appear hypocritical and an untrustworthy business partner if it turns on those nations which it has supplied, severely damaging future markets. This leads to friction between nations which should have a common interest in curtailing terrorism. A good example is the reluctance of Russia and China to impose strict sanctions on Iran, as both nations have strong economic ties to Tehran.

However, liberalism is an even wider term than realism and includes many theories less concerned with the beneficial effect of the free market under its umbrella. One of the most influential is institutional liberalism, known as idealism by some. This should not be confused with utopianism, although some realists do not draw the distinction. Liberal institutionalists prescribe a global organisation which can impose a system worldwide which will uphold peace and human rights. It can be traced back at least as far as Hugo Grotius, the so-called father of international law. Writing in the 17th Century[40], Grotius expanded on the far more ancient theory of natural law to claim that there were *universal* human rights which should bind states together. Later followers of Grotius and, again, Kant[41], in particular Woodrow Wilson and Hedley Bull, have added the more practical caveat that this can only be achieved through international institutions and the support of powerful nations. Sadly, liberal institutionalism has proved a chimera in practice: the most ambitious attempt to impose such a system (for the time), the League of Nations, can be at least indirectly blamed for the rise of the dictators in the 1930s which led to genocide on an almost unimaginable scale. As with structural realism, the value of liberal institutionalism is that it offers an explanation as to why the system fails. Ironically, the League of Nations was severely hindered by the US' inability to join (the Senate refusing to ratify the Treaty of Versailles which created the organisation) while today America views many developed countries as obstructionist toward its efforts to create an international consensus against Islamic terrorism. As with structural realism, liberalism fails to offer much guidance on how the situation can be rectified. As mentioned above, Grotian theory is severely hampered by its rather naïve assumption that some form of inalienable human right is acceptable to the majority of the global community. Even the most 'liberal' nations today are unable to establish any definitive human rights – debates over abortion, euthanasia and flag-burning are prime examples. When religion, tradition and nationalism are added to the mix, it is inconceivable that any such definitive international law could be imposed on states.

Keohane has taken up the challenge of applying modern liberal institutionalist theory to modern terrorism. In an article written in the weeks following the 9/11 attacks, he argues that "Global international organizations are potentially valuable resources in crises...in difficult times we can call upon them for support...If the United Nations Security Council did not exist, it would have to be invented...Without its continuing presence, our struggle against terrorism would be more difficult, and less likely to succeed." While the article focuses more on responses to, rather than causes of, terrorism, it is worth examining as Keohane focuses on the use of the UN to bring legitimacy to the responses to 9/11 such as the bombing of suspected Al-Qaeda training camps, which are often blamed as the cause of more recent attacks. Keohane argues that as the Council's "fifteen members currently include three Muslim countries - Bangladesh, Mali, and Tunisia... unanimous resolutions by the Security Council belie the claim that efforts against terrorism are "anti-Muslim."" However, it is submitted that this "legitimacy" is flawed in two major areas. Firstly, as the unofficial civil war in Iraq demonstrates, the schisms within Islam are often more bloody and divisive than between Islam and the Western world. In the tradition of liberal IR theorists Keohane is perhaps too eager to be distinguished from state-centric realist thought to consider how 'typical' his three examples are of the Muslim world. Bangladesh is a state where prior to a (secular) military coup, two women led the major parties (Begum Khaleda Zia and Sheikha Hasina), unthinkable in any fundamentalist Islamic nation; Tunisia is one of the most pro-Western nations in the Middle East, which has repressed and outlawed Islamic political movements, to the extent of sending police to toy shops to seize dolls with scarves[42], and is currently attempting to remove trade barriers with the EU; Mali is far more concerned with preserving its fragile democracy than global jihad and its troops regularly receive counter-insurgency training from the USA. The question which thus arises is what real value the vote of these three pragmatic nations is in "legitimising actions". One cannot argue that the legal status of abortion in a nominally Christian country such as the Netherlands is representative of the views of the Vatican! This leads into the second problem with Keohane's analysis – while UN-sponsored actions are certainly more widely supported among Americans and Europeans than those taken unilaterally[43], how far does their "legitimacy" affect those on the ground in nations such as Libya, Morocco, Iran and Pakistan? One of the most important aspects of fundamentalist terrorism is the pure hatred it exhibits. Those drawn to a *Jihad* against the West are unlikely to be turn away from violence simply because the UN authorised the bombing or the invasion or whichever other action provoked them into wishing to take direct and bloody retaliation.

Overall, liberalism would appear on closer inspection to forfeit its strengths in analysing non-state actors by focusing far too closely on Western norms and values. One commendable example to create a more relevant liberal approach and to move away from his own theories of institutional liberalism is provided in another recent article by Keohane[44] where he argues that liberal economic theories of "asymmetrical interdependence" can be applied, not only to military conflict, but to what he terms "informal violence", such as terrorist attacks. Asymmetrical interdependence in its original sense, as expressed by authors such as Nye[45] was not only economic in nature but often seen as a blessing, keeping potentially unruly states in line. Keohane (interestingly, a frequent co-author of Nye) turns this theory on its head by finding two areas in which Al-Qaeda had an asymmetrical interdependence over the United States – "information" and "belief". He argues that due to the openness of American society and its individualist, meritocratic nature, Al-Qaeda operatives were better informed about, and more motivated to damage, the USA than vice versa. The lesson to be learned is that "a state that is overwhelmingly powerful on many dimensions can be highly vulnerable on others...*we have over-emphasized states and we have over-aggregated power*".

Having given economic liberalism increased relevance, Keohane turns to liberal institutionalism. Here, his argument is rather less novel and has been rather overshadowed by the build-up to the invasion of Iraq yet it bears repeating. He contends that international organisations are vital to imbue any military action with legitimacy. In a *realpolitik* if not realist argument, Keohane explains that when the action demanded or legitimised by the global regime is popular, it obviously benefits leaders to win the approval of 'the world' for their decisions and where it is unpopular, it gives leaders an excuse to follow the policy in the face of domestic opposition. In fairness to Keohane, he admits that a possible action "such as an attack on Iraq...[may] not be legitimated...by the United Nations...Having acted unilaterally, the United States would not be moved to rely more heavily on international institutions, and multilateralism could suffer a serious blow".

Essentially this area of the argument, while strenuously protesting against such thinking, falls too easily into the liberal tradition of prescribing co-operation on the grounds that it would be in states' rational self-interest, without fully considering the many considerations which may preclude such co-operation. However, as Keohane correctly points out, many areas such as air travel are becoming increasingly globally governed as states see them as security threats rather than bureaucratic distractions. Whether this will lead to greater integration remains to be seen[46], and again this is merely a method of prevention rather than an explanation of the causes of terrorism.

Marxist theories: Is oppression always economic?

The following discussion will attempt to examine varying strains of thought under the same heading. They are related by their origin in the philosophies of Karl Marx. Some works separate these theories into different strands such as 'structuralism'[47], 'critical theory'[48] and 'class-system theory'[49] yet due to the overlap in ideas and theorists it is perhaps simpler and more efficient to deal with all of these in one section.

Of course Marx was not an international relations theorist, and the first theorist to fully apply Marxist economic theory to international relations was the British economist John Hobson who saw the exploitation of the workers by the bourgeoisie in the imperialist, 'jingoist' fervour of the times, as the European (and to some extent American, Russian and Japanese) nations increasingly relied on their foreign colonies for cheap labour and emerging markets. Hobson argued[50] that as the imperial nations developed, they increasingly faced unrest from the working classes (as predicted by Marx). In order to forestall a domestic socialist revolution, these states colonised weaker states, particularly in Africa and Latin America, to provide the underpaid labour capitalism requires to flourish. Of course, this led to increased and cheaper imports, which would be happily bought by the home country's working-class, further binding them to the existing class structure. It should be noted at this point that Leninist ideas of imperialism, while interesting and certainly not lacking in merit, focussed on the competition between the different imperialist states rather than the international class struggle.

Hobson and Lenin's ideas of imperialism were continued by the highly influential theorists who developed 'dependency theory'. This idea asserts that even in the post-colonial era, the first world (or 'North') continues to dominate the 'South' via indirect imperialism. This system of world capitalism maintains inequality, exploitation and uneven development. One of the prime examples is Latin America's relationship with the United States and it is no surprise that some of the most important dependency (or *dependencia* in the original Spanish) theorists, such as Cardoso and Prebisch, are Latin American. They pointed to the glaring disparity in the terms of trade between South and North America – the huge volumes of Latin American exports such as foodstuffs do not begin to pay for the far more expensive technological imports these countries require, such as computer chips and televisions.

This theory can be applied to the phenomenon of global terrorism in two ways. It can either be seen as the underlying cause of terrorism, or merely as the reason why terrorism is often poorly contained. The maximal approach would run that one of the main reasons for terrorist attacks such as 9/11 is that developing nations and their citizens are still denied any effective 'power' in the world system, be it military, diplomatic or economic. Terrorism is a low-cost, high-impact alternative. Speaking in the aftermath of the World Trade Center attacks, Noam Chomsky described it thus: "Terrorism works. It doesn't fail...They are telling us just what they think"[51]. Combs claims that "Today's terrorists tend to be drawn more from the less fortunate...terrorism represents the only way to lash out at society's injustices." For those impoverished or left landless or even stateless by 'globalisation', "The bitterness and frustration of this life of endless poverty...may well have produced the catalyst... For people who struggle to feed their families and feel left behind by economic globalization, the call to radicalism is powerful." Klare argues that "The creation of a global market has resulted in a growing divide... while globalization has improved living conditions in some areas, it has also increased the risk of conflict in others...This tendency is especially prevalent in parts of Africa, the Middle East, and Southeast Asia [the main hotbeds of terrorism], where economic growth has lagged behind other regions or has left some populations in a stagnant or declining position"[52]. Furthermore, for the modern state which wishes to achieve foreign policy goals without attracting the wrath of militarily superior nations (particularly the USA and, in the Middle East, Israel) "clandestine operations are, by their very nature, conducted in secrecy and consequently are often difficult to document...This makes the use of terrorism an attractive, but potentially dangerous, weapon for states seeking to carry out hostile acts without initiating a war"[53]. However, it can be assumed that outside of a few notable exceptions, such as Hezbollah, the majority of active terrorist threats are from stateless or revolutionary organisations, from Al-Qaeda to ETA.[54]

This leads to the more restrained application of dependency theory and its closely related cousin World Systems Theory (for which Wallerstein is generally credited) demonstrate why "peripheral" nations are unable, rather than unwilling, to devote the resources required to combating terror. Perhaps, as Marxist-based theories suggest, such governments lack the financial and logistical support to attack such 'cells'. If one does follow such a theory to its natural conclusion, then Western economic dominance might be said to be bought at a cost to its own security. Many living in the Third World would go even further and point to US interventionism, often through direct or indirect military force, as one of the major reasons many states are unable to offer strong resistance to terrorism taking root inside their borders. Whatever one's views on the 2003 invasion of Iraq, it is indisputable that the security situation has rapidly deteriorated since the removal of Saddam Hussein from power. Critics of structuralist theory argue that it is biased toward socialist theory and thus does not present a 'true' picture of the world. On a more practical level, liberal theorists point out that many of the *dependecia* methods of reforming the system have failed dramatically. More ideological criticisms focus upon the difficulties of categorising states under such broad labels as 'core' and 'periphery' and on whether the anti-imperialist explanations of structuralists are a more convincing explanation for the current world order than factors such as quality of leadership, geographic area and mere good fortune.

The previous paragraphs deal more with 'structuralist' theories, although as stated previously the margins are extremely blurred. Another strain of Marxist theory, loosely termed 'critical theory' concentrates more on the "humane" area of Marx's theories. It is a rather difficult doctrine to comprehend, as it mixes extremely realist views of the current world situation and hegemony with a far more liberal/socialist view of human nature as, if not essentially benevolent, at least susceptible to positive change. Critical theorists see a world 'structure' in a similar manner to that of Waltz, as a very vague outline in which actors operate.

However, they emphasise that while this structure constrains the behaviour of actors, the agents operating within the structure are far more diverse than merely sovereign states, and are able to change the overall norms of international society. Unsurprisingly, critical theorists have also explained the existence of any measure of structure in what they admit is fairly anarchical system, by the concept of hegemony. This is most clearly expressed in the works of the Italian communist Antonio Gramsci[55] who argues that while hegemony is the driving force behind the prevailing world structure at any point, the concept is wider than the hegemonic state (or states) identified by the neo-realists. Gramscian hegemony includes prevailing ideals and culture and this is of great importance to any discussion of US interests in the modern world, particularly related to terrorism. Whether or not the USA remains a hegemon in the realist sense following the Cold War is a hotly contested debate, yet it is far less controversial that there is a global Western hegemony of culture and ideology. Most former communist nations, such as those of Eastern Europe (and some states which remain at least nominally 'Communist' such as China) have readily adopted capitalism. Throughout the world Western culture ranging from rock music to fast food has in the space of decades displaced cultural traditions dating back millennia. In his famous essay 'Jihad vs. McWorld'[56], Benjamin Barber presciently wrote that "McDonald's in Moscow and Coke in China will do more to create a global culture than military colonization ever could."

Yet Gramsci also identifies a "counter-hegemony", made up of agents, be they individuals, NGOs, MNCs, states or international organisations, who wish to change the prevailing global structure. Gramscian theorists usually view such a movement as positive, believing this is the best method to combat both ancient and modern global woes, from torture to the threat of global warming. Some neo-Gramscian analysts such as Stephen Gill argue that "there is an urgent need for a counter-hegemony based on an alternative set of values, concepts and concerns…to deal with the problems of militarism and economic and social inequalities"[57]

At this stage in the analysis one is tempted to believe that Gramscian critical theory is perhaps the closest model to explaining events such as 9/11 and the London bombings. Unlike the realist approach it is able to take into consideration the various substate movements which are of far more relevance to the phenomenon of modern terrorism than states, yet it is also able to take a more neutral view of Western economic and political norms which are taken as dogma by liberals. Critical theorists are known for rejecting any one "truth" which can explain international relations. They believe (showing their Marxist roots) that the dominant social structure imposes certain beliefs on its members as "fact", which are in fact no more than value-laden judgements. Following this argument, as expanded by Habermas[58], counter-hegemonic forces can overturn such tenets.

However, when examining such an emotive issue as global terrorism, which raises concerns of national security at the highest level, there is a fundamental problem with this approach. Assuming that Islamic fundamentalism as interpreted by violent extremists can be said to be a relatively coherent body of thought which is clear as to its aim, is it therefore a counter-hegemony? It indisputably[59] seeks to overturn almost all what could be encompassed by 'Western culture', from democracy as a form of political organisation to moral standards such as the equality and liberation of women and ethnic minorities. Yet many of these goals are the entire opposite of what Gramscians expect from anti-hegemonic forces. They believe that such agents work towards what Linklater terms the "good society"[60], challenging practices which oppress people on grounds of class, race, gender etc. Are then US airstrikes and Guantanamo Bay the agents of freedom? Few critical theorists would wish to find themselves arguing such a view. Outside of rejecting critical theory outright, the only solution to this apparent paradox is to place the debate on international terrorism outside of the hegemonic structure, as an attempt to overthrow rather than modify the existing structure. In the words of Barber, "If the global future is to pit Jihad's centrifugal whirlwind against McWorld's centripetal black hole, the outcome is unlikely to be democratic"[61]. This may resolve the contradiction, but in its characterisation of Islam against the West leaves critical theorists dangerously close to deterministic and zero-sum perspectives such as those of Fukuyama, who famously declared that following the Cold War the world had reached "the end of history"[62].

Social Constructivism: Expanding sociology into high politics

Social constructivism is still a relatively new approach to International Relations and has been dismissed by more established theorists as a mish-mash of sociology, critical theory and post-modernism. However, before one can judge the efficacy of social constructivism a brief outline of its assumptions and goals and its relationship to IR is in order. Social constructivism is similar to critical theory in its emphasis on the absence of any universal "truth", instead seeing all "facts" about the world as a construct of ideology, experience and culture. However, it also goes much further in examining the role of culture and social identity. Critical theorists are content to leave this at what Marx termed 'unmasking', which was essentially to look past the established 'truth' to 'unmask' how it was constructed. In this approach the emphasis is upon the construction of knowledge to favour the existing capitalist system. Social constructivists, while acknowledging that 'truth' is a subjective concept, are more concerned with how such 'truths' are created and accepted, often at the subconscious level. A critical theorist would argue that the threat of Al-Qaeda is most likely exaggerated by the US government in order to maintain support for aggressive foreign policy, in an effort to unmask the 'truth' behind its stance. A social constructivist may accept this conclusion, that the threat of terrorist violence on American soil is lower than that represented, yet also argue that to the US government the threat is definitely genuine, placing his interest on why the US government perceives this as a threat when another nation (or a critical theorist) may not.

This is perhaps best expressed by Hacking in his illuminating work 'The Social Construction of What?'. He explains that "there need be no clash between construction and reality...concepts, practices, and people interact with each other. Such interaction is often the very point of social construction"[63]. Social constructivists do *not* deny the existence of terrorism nor that it is a major practical problem. What they are examining is the *construction* of terrorism by nations and people, rather than the reality. This may seem an unnecessary distinction but in fact leads in to the first important explanation offered by social constructivism. While the reality (such as the act, the number of casualties etc) of, for example, a suicide bombing of an Israeli settlement is an unchangeable fact for a Palestinian, an Israeli or a Norwegian, each person will interpret the event differently. Thus the Israeli will see an illegal 'terrorist' attack against innocent civilians; the Palestinian may characterise it as a legitimate act of resistance provoked by Israeli militarism; while the Norwegian may simply see it as the inevitable consequence of a region historically blighted by violence. All three observers have constructed a different "truth" of the same event. This process of interpretation and construction is beyond doubt – it is interesting to note that in a review of terrorist training facilities Combs complains of unreliable data as "the information was certainly biased... It is unlikely...that such an intelligence assessment [by another nation's intelligence service] would list "friendly" nations as hosts for terrorist camps, instead citing such camps as training sources for legitimate insurgent or revolutionary groups".[64]

It is submitted that this differing construction will impact the reality of terrorism in three separate areas. Firstly, there is the media. Terrorists have always had a particular relationship with the media – Frederick Hacker wryly commented "if the mass media did not exist, terrorists would have to invent them. In turn, the mass media hanker after terrorist acts because they fit into their programming needs...So there's a mutual dependency"[65]. How the media report the news is obviously of great importance to both the terrorists and the states they target. For a terrorist group, even if the reporting is negative, the aim is often simply to publicise their cause. For the state, obviously the aim is to delegitimise the violence and also to justify any actions taken by the state which could be blamed for inciting the terrorist act. Whether either of these goals is met is often due to the tone taken by the news media.

Related to this is the second impact of social construction as regards the current terrorist threat – the causes of terrorism and the recruitment of new members. It is one of the most ironic aspects of modern terrorism that as Western democracies struggle with growing voter apathy, particularly among the young[66], terrorist groups appear to have no problem recruiting members. It is even more surprising when the most 'popular' groups are of a religious nature, not traditionally seen as an area of great interest among teenagers and young adults. This poses the questions of how and why groups offering an early death and often little material reward appeal to so many above the chance to live a non-violent life. The answer overlaps considerably with the previous discussion of critical theory. 'Identity' is vital to terrorist groups. Only when they can impose the group identity upon a recruit will he then be receptive to the particular 'knowledge' of 'reality' that the group maintains. In the words of Combs: "The more…an individual perceives his or her identity in terms of the group of fellow terrorists, the less will be his or her ability to see the world as it really is…Remember too, that this group rejects the reality of laws as they currently exist and morality as it is defined by anyone except the group itself"[67]. Thus "to recruit effectively, groups must convey both legitimacy and identity, a clear sense of purpose and identity to those who might be seeking similar political goals".[68]

The London bombings in July 2005 provide the clearest example of why identity is so vitally important to the study of terrorist activity. All four of the suicide bombers were born in England and from the evidence collected by investigators and journalists, appear to have a background far removed from the 'typical' suicide bomber. For example, Mohammed Sidique Khan, whose bomb killed seven people as well as himself, was known in his hometown of Beeston as 'Sid'. School friends told journalists "The other Pakistani lads would have to go mosque because their families would say 'You're going to mosque.' But Sid didn't go…He didn't seem interested in Islam and I don't ever remember him mentioning religion."[69] Yet in his videotaped testament, aired on Al-Jazeera following the attacks, Khan stated: "I and thousands like me are forsaking everything for what we believe. Our driving motivation doesn't come from tangible commodities that this world has to offer. Our religion is Islam…I am directly responsible for protecting and avenging my Muslim brothers and sisters. Until we feel security, you will be our targets…We are at war and I am a soldier"[70]. This speech demonstrates both how Khan was drawn into a new identity as a fundamentalist Muslim, and how once inside that group he took on their construction of reality – as a "soldier" protecting his people rather than as a "terrorist" killing innocent people, Christians and Muslims alike.

Many commentators have simply blamed extremist preachers and associates who slowly 'convert' prospective bombers such as Khan. This may be the case, but again the same difficult question arises. Why does a person who has suffered little or no hardship, who has been brought up as a citizen of the United Kingdom and who in his formative years appeared almost dismissive of religion fall so suddenly and so absolutely under the spell of an extremist philosophy?

This phenomenon can be explained, but only by importing more ideas from sociology. Among social constructivists, Berger and Luckmann's work 'The Social Construction of Reality'[71] is seen as a seminal book in this area. The authors argue that every individual must, to some extent, become institutionalised and identify with a particular society or group at both an objective and a subjective level. For the purposes of the current subject, a discussion of the subjective level alone will suffice. Berger and Luckmann see two stages of 'socialisation' – primary and secondary. The primary stage is the most basic level, as a child learns about 'the world' in the sense of their immediate environment including communicating with others and understanding their reactions (be it by language or merely by understanding the meaning of expressions such as laughter). During "secondary socialisation", defined as "the internalization of institutional or institution-based 'sub-worlds'" individuals acquire "role-specific knowledge"[72]. This can be achieved with little emphasis on identity – for example the trainee secretary is unlikely to particularly identify with his or her typing school or with other secretaries.

However, as Berger and Luckmann note, "in some cases special techniques must be developed to produce whatever identification and inevitability are deemed necessary. The need for such techniques…may be posited for the sake of the vested interests of the personnel administering the socialization process in question." Now we are approaching the area of the 'terrorist mastermind', whether it is a wealthy backer such as Osama Bin Laden or a charismatic preacher. They continue, "The techniques applied in such cases are designed to intensify the affective change of socialization process. Typically, they involve the institutionalization…

in the course of which the individual comes to commit himself fully to the reality that is being internalized…He 'gives himself' to music, to the revolution, to the faith, not just partially but with what is subjectively the whole of his life. The readiness to sacrifice oneself is, of course, the final consequence of this type of socialization".[73] This is particularly true of violent extremists as "Terrorism is a group activity, involving intimate relationships among a small number of people. Interactions among members of the group may be more important in determining behaviour than the psychological predispositions of individuals… Terrorists can only trust each other. The nature of their commitment cuts them off from society; they inhabit a closed community."[74]

Thus it can be concluded that following the arguments of social constructivism, there is an understandable process by which a person can be, for want of a better word, 'resocialised'. Whether this is 'brainwashing' as some have alleged, or the rational choice of certain individuals, it is clear that 'identity' is by no means fixed, particularly when the original socialisation is of a far weaker nature. It will be discussed later as to how far the 'Western' or indeed 'British' socialisation process emphasises identity, and whether this ought to be altered. It is sufficient to say at this point, to paraphrase a famous post-modernist of a different ilk, Simone de Beauvoir, that a terrorist is not born but rather becomes a terrorist.[75]

Finally there is the impact of social construction upon responses to terrorism. As individuals can re-align their identity through the process of socialisation based upon experience, so arguably states can also be interpreted through social construction. For instance, Huntington, wrote almost a decade before 9/11 that in the wake of globalisation and ideas of the global village, many have reacted by identifying themselves far more closely with their home culture. This, in Huntington's opinion, leads to "cultural fault lines" which create "flash points for crisis and bloodshed". This constitutes one of the first attempts at a true examination of 'identity' as the catalyst for international conflict, albeit in couched in realist vocabulary.

Perhaps the most valuable product of this work was the response of Fukuyama and Barber who present a strong argument that Huntington is still incorrect in prophesising a cultural apocalypse. They argue that firstly, "Radical Islam has virtually no appeal in the contemporary world apart from those who are culturally Islamic to begin with"[76]. This ensures it cannot truly rival liberal capitalism as huge swathes of the globe, containing almost all of the most powerful countries (such as China and North America) have negligently small Muslim populations. Secondly, such extremism can be interpreted merely as an opportunity to restablish political principles as superior to unregulated and unchecked liberal economics – "a seminal moment…in which trauma opens up the possibility of new forms of action"[77]. While it can be (and has been) argued that Barber and Fukuyama also perhaps prioritise controversial absolutist conclusions over reasoned academic debate, their works remain an important check on overestimating the insights offered by social constructivism. There are advantages to viewing terrorism on a universalistic, geo-political level – one cannot become too enmeshed in the socialisation of individuals, nations or cultures without risking losing sight of the overall debate. As Hacker delightfully puts it, "Let us not throw out all cross-cultural babies when we take a historicist scrubrush to the universalist bath"[78].

This highlights one of the major problems with the social constructivist approach, which is that it can be very narrow, due to its sociological roots. While terrorism involves a far more individualist element than traditional IR subjects such as wars between nations, it can still be distinguished from the majority of areas of constructivist study due its political and global nature. A constructivist theorist may study, for example, a representative group of manual labourers in London and extrapolate from that a conclusion applicable to the nation, or, at a stretch, Europe. However, it is unlikely that he would claim this hypothesis applied across the globe. The problem is that if social constructivism is to offer a valid interpretation of global terrorism it must be capable of taking a broad approach which does apply worldwide. The enduring popularity of liberalism and realism derives from their applicability and application throughout space and time.

Conclusion:

The questions with which the paper begun must now be answered. Firstly, can international relations theory explain the causes of 9/11? The most mainstream approaches, liberalism and realism, appear rather unhelpful in this context. While realism recognises the inherent danger of war in the international system, it does not explain why groups such as Al-Qaeda which operate independently of any nation state would attack the USA. Liberalism is little better – by emphasising above all the economic factors which drive co-operation it fails to take account of those who do not see the free market and capitalism as progress. Furthermore, liberal calculations of rationality are normatively coloured by Western ideas, which lessen their value in analysing the behaviour of Muslim radicals. It could be said that through a realist or liberal perspective there is no distinction between Al-Qaeda, the Ku Klux Klan and the Cornish National Liberation Army[79].

A better explanation of the causes of 9/11 comes from critical theory. In his article on the attacks, Noam Chomsky[80] pinpoints three factors: (1) American support of Afghani militants during their war against Russia in the 1980s; (2) US hypocrisy in employing many methods which are "a very close paraphrase" of 'terrorism' in various conflicts; and (3) US policy in the Middle East, particularly with regard to support of the "harsh and brutal" Israel and military expansion in Saudi Arabia, home of Islam's holiest sites. Whether or not these were indeed the major motivations of the 9/11 hijackers, Chomsky's analysis highlights how such policies may, while advantageous to the West in realist military terms or liberal cost/benefit analysis (at least on a short-term basis), can cause great resentment when viewed on more humanist grounds. One must also include in this analysis the feminist and structuralist schools of thought, which emphasise the "arrogance" of the United States in conducting foreign policy and its dismissal, at least prior to 9/11, of peripheral states it did not see as a direct military threat. It also emphasises the role of globalisation, which has increasingly become synonymous in many people's minds with Americanisation. Finally, social constructivism offers an important insight into how a terrorist can be recruited and indoctrinated.

However, the most important question is what lessons can be learned. For realists, the answer is invasion of states which allow terrorists to operate within their borders. Yet considering the vast increase in terrorism both within Iraq and abroad following the invasion in 2003 (such as the London and Madrid bombings) this policy is at best flawed. Even in Afghanistan, initially heralded as an almost unqualified success[81], Taleban militants appear to have reclaimed much of the south of the country. The other traditional realist policy, deterrence, is of similar limited effect – the 9/11 bombers were not deterred by the fact that the US was (and remains) the most powerful military entity in history.

Classic liberals would argue that the solution is the extension of liberal ideology, both economic and political, to the nations and areas which are breeding grounds for terrorism. They argue that when the economic and, more importantly, democratic desires of these people are met, the necessity for violence steadily diminishes as they are able to achieve change through the ballot box and have more to lose by creating conflict, as they are tied into the interdependent world economy. Leaving aside the economic difficulties (of extending the trade and transport links to such areas and the fact that in many such areas (for example Palestine) there is a lack of any real products with which to trade) there are three major problems with democracy 'for export'. Firstly there are the obvious logistical and social difficulties with imposing a new form of political organisation on nations with a very different historical tradition. Nations which are 'democratic' in name only already abound, examples ranging from Egypt[82] to Nigeria[83]. However, there is also a further issue even if democracy is successfully established. As first Europe and subsequently the world found to its cost between 1933 and 1945, where the conditions are right, democracy can bring the most violent and abhorrent political movements to power as easily as a coalition of liberal centrists[84]. In the most extreme regions of the world, where terrorism thrives, many of the ideas which it espouses would be no more palatable and indeed often far more destructive if implemented by an elected administration. Governments could be committed to war with Israel in the Middle East or the genocide of entire tribal groups in Africa. This ties in with the third problem, that democracy can also simply enhance the schisms within divided areas. In Iraq the administration has merely demonstrated the split between Sunni, Shi'ite and Kurdish Iraqis, with each government department hijacked for use in these ethno-political rivalries. Palestine is another demonstration of this problem – following the 2006 election which brought Islamist Hamas to power[85], the split with secular Fatah has widened to the extent that the Palestinian territories have, in political terms, split in two, with Hamas holding the Gaza Strip while Fatah rule the West Bank.

Liberal institutionalists are at least able to offer up the idea of a global organisation with which to combat such issues. While an excellent idea with which to legitimise and empower the war against terrorism, it suffers from the same problem which effectively negates all such institutional solutions – the lack of effective global co-operation. The coalitions assembled to invade Afghanistan and Iraq included only a small number of states as effective members and have already suffered serious discord (such as Spain withdrawing following the Madrid bombings). The UN is yet to even agree on a definition of "terrorism", a prerequisite for any international action against global terror.

Again more innovative solutions arise from the less mainstream approaches. While most Marxian rooted ideals remain staunchly utopian and have little practical relevance and others such as structuralism highlight the problems of combating terrorism without providing any detailed explanation of the causes of radicalisation, critical theory does offer some light on the subject. Just as the US was counselled (unsuccessfully) to win the "hearts and minds" of the Vietnamese, again today if the West were able to stir peaceful counter-hegemonist sentiment in the areas where that hegemony consists of radical Islam[86], theoretically the urge for emancipation would be a powerful ally. However, policy makers would do well to remember the origins of the phrase, in a quote of John Adams, second president of the United States, who wrote "The Revolution was effected before the War commenced. The Revolution was in the minds and hearts of the people; a change in their *religious* sentiments of their duties and obligations" [italics added for emphasis]. Others note that structuralists have provided valuable stimuli for the major economically powerful nations of the world to realise that "the economic divide is huge and getting wider" and that this has provoked "a search for solutions of a more realistic and permanent nature"[87] in areas such as the UN Millennium Development Goals and the decision in 2005 (ironically the same weekend as the London bombings) of the G8 summit to double aid to Africa.

However, it is submitted that again one must return to social constructivism when attempting to find an explanation as to why global terrorism continues to grow in the face of the realist and liberal 'solutions' outlined above. This is a pre-requisite to finding a long-term solution to reduce terrorism in a more conclusive manner than killing existing terrorists, a solution which will staunch the flow of recruits to terrorist organisations. It would appear to be generally accepted within the academic community that the current dominant form of terrorism differs in some fundamental aspects from earlier movements. Rapoport distinguishes four such waves over the previous century, from the almost genteel terror of the middle-class anarchists to modern religious fundamentalism. He identifies the "fourth wave" as having a "recruitment pattern unique in the history of terrorism…In the past every terrorist *organization* recruited from a single national base or people". The importance of social constructivism comes in trying to explain the widening of the support base for terrorism. Of course homeless and landless Palestinians will be tempted to support extremist Palestinian organisations who promise them a better future. But why are so many Muslims, even those with an affluent and seemingly content life in stable areas, turning to the cause of radical Islam? Many explanations and solutions have been posited, often flatly contradicting one another. In just one section of one contemporary collection of writings by distinguished academics on terrorism, the relationship of Islam to terror is variously characterised as: 1) irrelevant, in an article by Wilkinson "As in earlier periods of history, religious fanaticism and terror are not the exclusive preserve of any single major religion…It is…absurd to equate mainstream Islamic religion with the terrorism

71

committed by extremist groups acting in the name of Islamic beliefs."[88]; 2) as an excuse for more political motives in the view of Crenshaw "although often justified in terms of religious principle, its roots lie in American support for regimes with embittered domestic oppositions"[89]; and 3) as the driving force by Lewis "This is no less than a clash of civilizations – the perhaps irrational but surely historical reaction of an ancient rival against our Judeo-Christian heritage, our secular present, and the worldwide expansion of both"[90]. This is a small example of the contradictions inherent in this area. For the purposes of this article it is sufficient to say that the terrorist attacks referred to and analysed were characterised as Islamic by those who carried them out. It is submitted that the issue is not Islam as a religion, but Islam as an identity.

What then is the fundamentalist Islamic identity? It is by no means a cohesive doctrine but rather a collection of ideas, statements and mindsets which at first appeal to potential recruits, and can then be used to further indoctrinate them into the cause. It encompasses many of the traditional justifications for terrorist violence, such as vengeance, the lack of alternatives and the belief that one is acting "on behalf of a majority unaware of its plight".[91] This is combined with fundamentalist interpretations of religious doctrine which, it is submitted, is the most important area of the constructed identity. The current wave of terror is unique in attracting recruits globally and extreme Islam is one of the most effective methods of doing this. While many (particularly those who already possess a more balanced education in that religion) are immune to these pleas, there are plenty of potential recruits, particularly among the young, the poor and the uneducated, who can be swayed by the 'word of God'. An appeal to a higher being is a powerful tool and as history has shown time and time again can override purely national identities. Thus the Crusaders rode out British and French alike, despite the Crusades marking one of the few periods of the surrounding centuries when the two nations were not at war. It is argued that modern radical Islam is even more useful to recruiters as it not only can override the identity of being 'British' or 'American' etc., but it can also override the identity of being a moderate Muslim. Thus in the 'testimony' of another of the London bombers, Shehzad Tanweer, he complains that "Muslims of Britain, you, day in and day out, on your TV sets watch and hear about the oppression of the Muslims, from the East to the West. But yet you turn a blind eye and carry on with your lives as if you never heard anything, or as if it does not concern you...You have preferred the *dunyaa* [the tangible commodities of the world] to Allah and His Messenger". This also makes it easier for the terrorist to kill those of his own people and even of his own faith and still retain the belief that is he is doing good. While a rather idiosyncratic view, it should perhaps be noted that in Feshback's dichotomy this is exacerbated by the militant Islamic identity being 'nationalist' rather than 'patriotic'.[92]

In addition to this, it can also be argued that Europe is currently undergoing something of an identity crisis. Again taking the United Kingdom as an example, those who in the previous decades would have unerringly identified themselves as British are now unsure of how to define themselves. At one level, as the European Union grows ever larger and extends across greater and greater areas of policy, it would appear that a loss of identity is occurring from above. Yet at the other time, as devolution has been followed by increasingly rumblings from Scotland of wanting full autonomy to exploit her lucrative gas deposits and from England of becoming tired of shouldering the tax burden for much of the welfare paid out north of the border, it would appear that identity is becoming increasingly localised. Indeed, both inhabitants of the largest cities and the most isolated communities seem to increasingly identify at a sub-national level – either due to multiculturalism (as in London, Birmingham etc.) or due to their own more historical cultural differences (such as the revival of calls for Cornish independence as a Celtic nation). It is unsurprising that when even those whose ancestors have been 'British' for 300 years since the Acts of Union are unsure of their identity, more recent immigrants are wont to fall under identities which resonate from their homeland.

The British have always traditionally been rather bemused by the American form of patriotism, seeing it as rather brash and jingoistic. Even in the days of Empire flags were to be flown from official buildings, not in front of every house. In the aftermath of terrorist attacks on America many were quick to blame the 'arrogance' of the USA, not least in the "my country, right or wrong" approach which is at the forefront of American identity. However, following the 7/7 bombings it is suggested that many have taken a rather new appraisal of the American system. Without entering the vast arguments concerning the 'melting pot' approach to immigration as opposed to European methods of multiculturalism, it can be said that the sight of hundreds of thousands of illegal Central American immigrants waving the Stars and Stripes protesting for the right to citizenship[93] is a rather different one to those of thousands of British-born Muslims protesting against the UK government and encouraging suicide bombing.

This is not to suggest that American attitudes are any more effective in creating a more integrated identity in the vast majority of citizens than British, as this argument can be easily disposed of by pointing to, amongst other things, the difference in immigration patterns into each nation, the happy integration of a large majority in the UK and America's own struggles with domestic terrorism such as the Oklahoma City bombing. However, it does suggest that at some point the British or English identity has been subsumed by others in a way that has not occurred in America. Much of this is due to increasingly bizarre attempts by recent governments to implement 'political correctness' in the most inflexible and authoritarian manner possible. As the first waves of major immigration reached Britain in the 1950s and 1960s, it is undeniable that these new arrivals faced (and in some case still do face) unacceptable levels of racism, often at an institutional level. However, since that period and increasingly through the previous fifteen years, the response of the government has been to concentrate on the form rather than the substance of the problem. It is submitted that initiatives such as avoiding the word 'Christmas' and reclassifying British-born citizens into ever smaller 'ethnic minorities' are counter-productive – they separate rather than integrate and are fuel for the fire of extremists on both sides of the chasm. While the approach taken in nations such as America is perhaps insufficiently sensitive toward important cultural differences, it cannot be denied that 'multiculturalism' as interpreted by successive British governments has increasingly ghettoised many minority groups. Evidence of this argument is always controversial; however one interesting point is the response of the first-generation immigrant parents of the London bombers. All four were appalled at their son's actions and eager to emphasise their own commitment to the country. This is an indicator of a prevailing and worrying trend – those born in modern Britain feel less of an affinity to the nation than those who immigrated from elsewhere, who were faced with far less tolerance and began with few economic resources. A recent article in the Economist also pointed out that the phenomenon is not confined to Muslims – "In Britian, even more than in America, Israel is an anchor of Jewish identity. Britons are far more likely to have visited Israel, have family there and call themselves Zionists [than Americans]"[94]

It is again to be stressed that this is merely an example and that the underlying point is true of nations with a far different approach than the United Kingdom. The conclusion is that, as social constructivists have discovered, even in a relatively simple society with a strong common identity, such as a tribal village, "unsuccessful socialization into one social world may be accompanied by successful socialization into another"[95]. This is the first step toward radicalisation. The would-be rebel fails to find sufficient identity in his home village and becomes receptive to a different belief. Once this has occurred, "a cleavage appears between 'appearance' and 'reality' in the individual's self-apprehension." He may still appear a 'nice boy' or a 'good man' possessing qualities prized by the society in question, such as courtesy or a strong work-ethic. However, in his own mind he has already become separated from this society. The eventual result is that "one will no longer be sure whether an individual so defined identifies himself in the same way or not…it will no longer be an easy matter to recognize anyone's identity". Thus a climate of confusion and fear can arise, leading to further problems in the original socialisation process which will then produce more who fail to identify.

In a more complex web of identities, such as in a modern industrial society, there are more problems at the outset. "Unsuccessful socialization may also result from the mediation of acutely discrepant worlds by significant others during primary socialization…the individual is presented with a choice of profiled identities…He may become a man as understood by race *A* or as understood by race *B*". At this point, as Berger and Luckmann note, even the child's own parents may not realise that he has chosen the 'other' identity.

How then ought this to be addressed? Clearly the problem is that the socialisation at primary level has seen the individual take the 'wrong' course of action. Thus moves must be made to ensure that the desired identity is the logical choice. Of course there will still be those who are indoctrinated by a particularly influential figure, however, Berger and Luckmann argue that where the concept of alternate realities arises at a secondary level "internalization need *not* be accompanied by affectively charged identification with significant others; the individual may internalize different realities *without* identifying with them".

However, primary level socialisation is, as already stated, seen as the most basic level of socialisation, where one learns about one's parent's or guardian's world. Thus the logical next step to explain those who fail to take a relativist view of secondary socialisation is that the first world they experience is insufficiently clear to provide a solid enough primary socialisation. This produces a situation similar to the earlier example of the simple society. The individual is never primarily socialised, even though he may appear to be so. He has already failed to internalise it in his mind, so when he is presented with multiple realties at a later stage of development he is incapable of relativity, lacking any point of comparison. Thus rather than realising that his parent's world is not the same as the world described by the fundamentalist preacher or other significant other and being able to compare both, he has already rejected the earlier world and if the new reality offered is sufficiently persuasive, will accept it as unquestioningly as a small child successfully internalises primary socialisation.

It is not surprising then that those who have provided the most obvious example of this process, the London bombers, were the children of immigrants loyal to their adopted country. Faced with not only the weak 'British' identity which claimed to incorporate those of a non-Anglo Saxon ethnicity while continually differentiating them but also their parents own confused identity in a foreign land, where their original identity as Asians faced the "threat" of dilution it is clear that for some the primary socialisation process would fail.

Add to this the sociological research which has found that "identity threat accentuates group distinctiveness in the context of a larger society or organization. This cycle may be accentuated in periods of widespread social uncertainty…People are often seen to be more committed in their identification with their group's belief systems…At the extreme, identification with "totalist" groups can translate into atrocities".

Following the social constructivist argument to its end would thus produce a solution which can be easily summarised: to prevent the indoctrination of would-be terrorists, they must be given a strong enough identity and reality to internalise as part of their primary development. It is not essential that they unquestioningly accept this reality, indeed, this is highly unlikely. They must simply be able to comprehend, by the time they are faced with highly conflicting realities, that no one reality, least of all an extreme, is the 'truth'.

THE CURRENT STANDING OF FREEDOM OF EXPRESSION, THOUGHT, CONSCIENCE AND RELIGION IN THE SPECIAL ADMINISTRATIVE REGION OF HONG KONG UNDER INTERNATIONAL LAW

By Matthew W. Proud LL.B (Hons.) LL.M

Editor's note: The following article is a condensation of the results of Matthew Proud's investigation into human rights in Hong Kong

Introduction

Since the end of British rule more than a decade ago, Human Rights in Hong Kong have been brought significantly under the international spotlight. The objectives of this paper are to examine the standing of the rights to freedom of expression, thought, conscience and religion in Hong Kong today.

For the purpose of this article, freedom of thought, conscience and religion can include "freedom to change religion or belief and freedom, either alone or in community with others and in public or in private, to manifest religion or belief, in worship, teaching, practice and observance"[96]. Freedom of expression is taken to mean the ability to express oneself free of censorship and to include freedom of the press.

Freedom of Thought, Conscience and Religion

Under international law freedom of thought, conscience and religion are legally binding on all member states who are signatories to the International Covenant on Civil and Political Rights (ICCPR), under Article 18 of the covenant; Britain signed on behalf of Hong Kong and the Hong Kong Bill of Rights Ordinance was later enacted giving effect to the ICCPR domestically. Post-handover, it appears on the surface that Mainland China's government policy of limiting worship to a regulated system of registered mainstream faiths has not been implemented into Hong Kong. Nevertheless, documented cases of religious discrimination and prosecution by the authorities in the former territory occur; thus contrasting the freedoms the peoples of Hong Kong enjoyed under colonial British rule. These documented cases illustrate the deteriorating state of these freedoms in Hong Kong today. This recent trend has raised the question of the sustainability of the rule of law in Hong Kong. This is because these rights are thought to be protected domestically under the Basic Law, Article 32.

The importance of freedom of thought, conscience and religion is thought to be paramount to most other freedoms; the maintenance of such freedoms is non-negotiable according to the international community. The United Nations Human Rights Commission has found that "These freedoms are [to be] protected unconditionally", their findings went on to specify that these rights "cannot be derogated from"[97] under any circumstances. The consequence of these findings is colossal in its effect. By elevating these freedoms above others the Commission has in essence quashed the exploitation and use of the defense of "cultural relativism" as a justification for governments to derogate from covenant rights. Because Hong Kong is a signatory to the ICCPR (considered by some legal experts to be international customary law) it would be impossible and clearly unlawful for the government of Hong Kong to try and derogate from covenant rights using cultural relativism as a justification. The authorities cannot claim that the fundamental rights of thought, conscience and religion are European values not Chinese and therefore do not need to be adhered to.

Despite the Hong Kong government doing an adequate job most of the time in protecting freedom of thought, conscience and religion in Hong Kong, when these rights have been infringed, the overall majority of the cases involves and surrounds the treatment of the religious movement, know as Falun Gong.

Falun Gong

Described by former HKSAR Chief executive Tung Chee, as "a mixture of [an] evil sect and political group" that "his government must guard against"[98], followers of Falun Gong have found their rights violated as they fall victim to the political pressure placed on the HKSAR from the Mainland. Chee's statement alone could be seen to amount to a violation of the ICCPR under Article 20(2), the prohibiting of any advocacy of national, racial or religious hatred that constitutes incitement to discrimination, hostility or violence.

The two paramount areas of concern, with violations of these rights are by means of discrimination through immigration entry control and through political pressure:

(a) *Discrimination through immigration entry control*

There have been multiple reports of practicing members of the Falun Gong religion being denied entry into Hong Kong.[99][100] The government of the HKSAR has taken the position that a state has the right to control the entry of non-nationals into its territory and in Hong Kong this power is devaluated to the HKSAR under the Basic Law. *Prima facie* this principle is correct and legally sound, as the Hong Kong Bill of Rights Ordinance does state that the ICCPR *"does not affect any immigration legislation governing entry into, stay in and departure from Hong Kong"*[101]. However, the purpose of human rights law, along with the spirit of the ICCPR, is to ensure that individuals are protected from the potentially negative impact of states' policy. It can be submitted that Article 18 of the ICCPR; right to freedom of thought, conscience and religion; has attained *jus cogens* status. The importance of this right was emphasised by the US Supreme Court in the case of *Palko v Connecticut (1937)* where the justices found that without the concept of freedom of thought all other freedoms are seemingly meaningless[102]. This judicial statement gives tremendous force to this age-old concept, which dates back to biblical times[103].

It can be suggested that the Hong Kong government's judgment is inaccurate in its interpretation of the ICCPR, which is given force domestically through the Hong Kong Bill of Rights Ordinance and the Basic Law. The Hong Kong Bill of Rights Ordinance – which the government points to for its source of law on being able to discriminate against people on grounds of thought, conscience and religion, when determining whom can enter the HKSAR – states that under Article 13:

'An alien lawfully in the territory of a State Party to the present Covenant may be expelled therefrom only in pursuance of a decision reached in accordance with law and shall, except where compelling reasons of national security otherwise required, be allowed to reasons against his expulsion and to have his case reviewed by...the competent authority"

In addition, the Basic Law, states under Article 41, that:

"Persons in the Hong Kong Special Administrative Region other then Hong Kong residents, shall in accordance with law enjoy the rights and freedoms of Hong Kong residents."

Furthermore, the ICCPR makes clear under Article 4(1) that only:

"In time of public emergency which threatens the life of the nation and the existence of which is officially proclaimed, the States Parties to the present Covenant may take measures derogating from their obligations under the present Covenant to the extent strictly required by the exigencies of the situation, provided that such measures are not inconsistent with their other obligations under international law"

Article 4(1) goes on to hold that even when a state must, for the sake of pure necessity, derogate from the covenant right, in doing so they may not:

"involve (in) discrimination solely on the ground of race, colour, sex, language, religion or social origin"

The Hong Kong government has failed to understand that, firstly, under the ICCPR they are only able to deny people the right of appeal in times of emergency and even in times of emergency they may not discriminate solely on the ground of religion. Secondly, the Basic Law applies to non-residents also, just as the Human Rights Act, which gives effect domestically to the European Convention of Human Rights, does in the UK. Therefore, the government may not preclude people from entering Hong Kong on grounds of religion or social origin, as they have done to practitioners of Falun Gong.

The government's reliance domestically on the Hong Kong Bill of Rights Ordinance as reason for exclusion is flawed as well. This is because in common law jurisdictions the doctrine of implied repeal means that successive legislation will take precedence over the previous legislation. Therefore, when determining grounds for who qualifies for entry into Hong Kong the Basic Law repeals all portions of the Hong Kong Bill of Rights Ordinance which are contradictory. Consequently, because the Basic Law gives effect to the ICCPR, the correct approach the government should have taken was to interpret the Basic Law and the ICCPR when endeavouring to preclude a specific group of people on the basis of their membership of a particular religious or social organisation. This would have failed due to the fact that it is contrary to both sources of law. It can therefore be submitted that the government in barring Falun Gong form entering Hong Kong has acted unlawfully.

Even without formulating freedom of thought, conscience and religion in legal language or as a legal concept, it appears on the face of it to be most unfair and indeed against the spirit, if not the letter, of the ICCPR to have individuals discriminated against due to their religious beliefs when being determined entry into the region. If people are being discriminated against for their religious beliefs clearly they do not have freedom of thought, conscience and religion. Under international law this is an unlawful practice, which is contradictory juxtaposed to colonial rule.

(b) *Violations through political pressure*

In the spring of 2002 members of the Falun Gong spiritual group were arrested for protesting in Hong Kong and accused of obstruction and assault[104]. After a lower court convicted the protestors, animosity began to spread among civil liberty advocates against the restriction of freedoms guaranteed by China upon reunification with the former colony. It was suggested that Article 21 and 22 of the ICCPR, regarding the rights to peaceful assembly and freedom of association were being violated. The Hong Kong Bar Association also found in its submission on *The Right of Peaceful Assembly or Procession* that:

> "It is of fundamental importance that such legal regimes [the government] should not be so overbearing as to have the effect of stifling or threatening any exercise of such rights."

Moreover, the Bar Association pointed out that the rights to peaceful assembly and freedom of association were basic constitutional rights, which was decided over a hundred years ago, and although there are restrictions on it, at common law, it was made clear by O'Brian J, in *R v Londonderry* (1881)[105] that:

> "If danger arises from the exercise of lawful rights resulting in

a breach of the peace, the remedy is the presence of sufficient force to prevent the result, not the legal condemnation of those who exercise these rights."

Furthermore, the Bar Association made clear that "any restrictions on the right of assembly must be necessary". They went on to point out that 'necessary' "is not the same as convenient or expedient." And it should be understood that a "fundamental distinction [is drawn] between restriction and suppression of a right". The point is that it can hardly been seen by the reasonable man, using an objective standard of the highest order, that the Hong Kong sect of Falun Gong, which is "barely 500 members, most [of whom are] middle-aged… [and whom] at dawn, gather in parks to practice their meditation and breathing exercises"[106], threaten any real breach of the peace in Hong Kong by exercising their right of peaceful assembly or procession. It appears form the outset in this case that the prosecution of Falun Gong has nothing to do with a breach of the peace and instead is about the groups "legal condemnation…[for] exercis[ing] these rights[107]", by the Chinese government because that they wish to silence them for protesting against China's human rights record[108], particularly when objectively taking into account the actuality that in Mainland China individuals are imprisoned for "engaging in Falun Gong practices, but also for merely admitting that they adhere to the teaching"[109], (in essence the ultimate violation of a person's freedom of thought) and that statements from the highest levels of the post-handover Hong Kong government speak of the practices in a loathsome manner.

How can an objective mind not come to the conclusion that the government of the HKSAR are, under pressure from the central government, doing anything short of publicly admitting to suppress Falun Gong's rights to freedom of thought, conscience, religion, expression and peaceful assembly?

Due to the heavy-handed opposition to the spiritual group from Beijing it appears that this was a political maneuver. It is a fundamental principle of human rights that a tribunal deciding on someone's fate should act independently and impartially[110], therefore if any pressure was being put on the courts by the central government then it would be a violation of individuals' civil liberties, as well as an infringement of Article 85 of the Basic Law[111]. Rights activists questioned the perception of political interference into the judiciary. However, in May 2005 the final appeal court quashed the convictions citing that they based the decision on constitutional rights to demonstrate and to engage in free speech[112]. This indirectly demonstrated that the judiciary in Hong Kong is still just as willing as it was under British rule to uphold the rule of law and protect constitutional rights such as the rights to peaceful assembly and freedom of association, especially when they co-exist with freedom of thought, conscience and religion as they undoubtedly did in this case.

In Hong Kong the executive branch's vocal support for the policies of Beijing, especially under Chief Executive Tung Chee, coupled with various judicial decisions all the way up to the final appeal court created a political anxiety, which surrounded constitutional rights. In the future any further intervention in the way of political pressure from Beijing, which breaches constitutional rights protected by law, may lead to the unwinding of the current stability and rule of law inherited from the British and currently enjoyed in Hong Kong.

Without a doubt, political pressure from Beijing on Hong Kong will not disappear anytime soon. It is the nature of political system in Mainland China to try to impose their political culture of repression on Hong Kong. Optimistically the judiciary will continue to uphold basic human rights in Hong Kong.

Freedom of Expression

Freedom of expression is accepted as a Human Right and is protected under Article 19 of the ICCPR and Article 19 of the Universal Declaration of Hunan Rights. Freedom of expression is considered to be the ability to express oneself free of censorship and it includes freedom of the press. In Europe the courts have declared that freedom of expression constitutes part of the essential foundation of a democracy[113], especially when concerned with freedom of the press[114]. While freedom of expression does have its limits even in the most liberal of societies, such as hate speech, perjury, contempt of court and defamation, it should only have restrictions placed on it when the courts have given the most careful scrutiny[115].

In Hong Kong freedom of expression is protected under the Basic Law Article 27 and 34. However, this has not stopped the government from trying to restrict these freedoms. In 2002, in an attempt to give the government more power, the HKSAR announced plans to implement the National Security (Legislative Provisions) Bill to implement Article 23 of the Basic Law into the legislative books. Article 23 states:

> "The Hong Kong Special Administrative Region shall enact laws on its own to prohibit any act of treason, secession, sedition, subversion against the Central People's Government, or theft of state secrets, to prohibit foreign political organizations or bodies from conducting political activities in the Region, and to prohibit political organizations or bodies of the Region from establishing ties with foreign political organizations or bodies"[116]

This created outrage among the public for fear that the new law would invoke the notion of treason against any political organization that was banned by the Central government for not agreeing with them in certain circumstances. Furthermore, that the proposed law would erode freedom of speech rights. In July 2003, an estimated 500,000 people took to the streets to protest the new law, which would implement Article 23.[117] This resulted in the government withdrawing the legislation.

Although there have been isolated violations of this human right, if viewing freedom of expression in Hong Kong from a broad spectrum, it can be submitted that it has been well protected under Chinese control. Furthermore, academic freedom is protected under law making Hong Kong home some of Asia and the world's top universities[118]. Most issues involving infringement of Freedom of Expression have to do with restriction in the press.

(c) *Freedom of the Press*

In recent years there have been a number of alarming incidents surrounding freedom of the press in Hong Kong. These incidents have ranged from the March 2006 alleged attacks on a newspaper, "when four men armed with hammers broke into the office of the Epoch Times, a newspaper known for criticizing the Chinese Communist Party and reporting on Falun Gong[119]." to the more prominent practice of self-censorship. Freedom of the press is protected under Article 27 of the Basic Law. However, this has not stopped the political players in Beijing from attempting to obstruct this freedom.

(d) *'Newsgathering' & The Protection of Journalistic Sources*

Domestically, an area of contentiousness has been the right of "newsgathering" - this is because it has not been: "explicitly protected in either the Hong Kong Basic Law or the International Covenant on Civil and Political Rights. Nor has the scope of the right of newsgathering ever been properly defined by the courts."[120] It should be noted that there are basic areas of newsgathering which are restricted in most common law jurisdictions, such as: entry to private property and certain public places such as government buildings and military instillations and certain criminal investigations and trials, along with restrictions imposed for public order reasons. The lack of law governing this area creates a gray area where an executive is potentially able to place further limits on the ability of journalists to gather news. Because there is no authoritative statement of the law regulating this, the burden is now on the judiciary to create precedents to protect this fundamental freedom.

Along with the protection of newsgathering, the protection of journalistic sources is not adequately protected. Hong Kong, unlike the United Kingdom, does not have any statutory protection against this kind of disclosure.[121] Indeed, "at common law, journalists do not have any immunity to preserve the confidentially of their sources."[122] However, the courts have not been keen to grant requests for disclosure of sources[123]. If heavy political pressure is applied from Beijing these two areas may come under attack from the HKSAR government. Once again the judiciary must act now at common law to create the necessary precedence to offer these protections to the media.

(e) *Self-censorship*

Human Rights Watch has reported that self-censorship is prevalent in the media within Hong Kong, particularly with coverage of mainland issues[124]. It is still an outstanding problem with reporting in the SAR as well. It has been submitted that the Chinese authorities exert their influence by use of a three-part approach: punishment; rewards and public relations[125]. A good example of punishment is that of the Daily Apple, a Chinese language newspaper, owned by Jimmy Lai, whom held views hostile to the Chinese government and was extremely critical of the Tiananmen Square incident. Not only was it reported that The Daily Apple was constantly denied entry in to China in February 1997, but when Mr. Lai was taking his company public on the stock exchange all backers pulled their support overnight. Twelve banks all cited the reason in doing so to be political pressure[126].

Furthermore, Chinese controlled companies have in the past been banned from advertising in non-friendly media outlets.[127] When applying the mechanism of rewarding media outlets, standard procedure is to allow media access into the mainland. In addition the Chinese are masterminds at using propaganda to silence non-friendly voices in the press. Undoubtedly this constitutes an implied violation of Article 19 of the ICCPR along with Article 27 of the Basic Law, freedom of the press. Self-censorship on media coverage in Hong Kong is extremely contentious. A resent poll by the University of Hong Kong, which was published in the South China Morning Post in November 2005, found that nearly half of Hong Kong's people believe the local news media has practiced self-censorship. [128] In addition nearly thirty percent of journalists admitted to partaking in self-censorship.[129]

It seems apparent that as long as self-censorship seems to be working then there is no need for further formal restrictions to the freedom of the press. It has been submitted that as long as the Chinese authorities are satisfied that: "no advocacy for the independence of Hong Kong and Taiwan; no advocacy for subverting Chinese rule; [and no] personal attacks on Chinese leaders[130]" are ahead to then "press freedom in Hong Kong should be maintained[131]", with respect to all other areas of reporting.

Conclusion

The promise for the continuation of the system of government previously enjoyed under British rule clearly has not been kept in Hong Kong. Unfortunately the basic human rights of freedom of expression, thought, conscience and religion have been unlawfully violated under both international and domestic law. All of these violations have taken place regardless of the obligations undertaken by Hong Kong and China under international law.

The decline of civil liberties in Hong Kong since the end of British rule, were previously expected before the handover of the British colony to communist China in 1997. It seems apparent that the lessons learned from this social experiment of "one country, two systems" can be that whenever people are the subjects of an authoritarian government, no matter what precautions are put in place, human rights will regrettably deteriorate.

Perhaps one of the largest disappointments has been the poor response on the behalf of the international community. Apart from a few critical statements periodically from Western governments and NGO's the issue of declining human rights seems to go unnoticed. Sadly, although, Hong Kong is no longer part of the West, it seems extremely disingenuous that we allow civil liberties in this region to decline because the international community either does not care or is interested in appeasing China for other reasons.

Optimistically, in the future the judiciary will continue to do its best to try and limit the power of the executive branch and thus the desires of the government in Beijing. Moreover, if the road to democracy continues and elections are allowed on the grounds of universal and equal suffrage, to go ahead as planed by the end of the next decade, the destiny of the peoples of Hong Kong will finally be in their own hands. However, in the not so distant future, more animosity will develop because China, as agreed upon with Britain, is only obligated to preserve the laws and a high degree of autonomy in Hong Kong for fifty years after the transfer.

DEFINING AND APPLYING THE 'CULTURAL PRINCIPLE'

By Dinesh C. Rajp LL.B (Hons.) LLM

Editor's note: The following extract is a continuance of Dinesh Rajp's pursuit for the development of a 'cultural principle' in law. The principle was borne of the writer's initial thoughts set out in his Masters of Law thesis. This chapter considers its relevence, to not only historical events, but indeed within the modern context.

Philosophical Foundations and Other Concepts

To interpret and explore human rights discourse, one must enquire into: in the first, the philosophical concept of epistemology, or the theory of knowledge and in the second, the concept of culture. These two conceptual foundations are imperative to human rights' assessments and their very existence within their infrastructure queries the *universality* of rights per se.

The relevance of epistemology and culture will be explored on three fundamental levels. In the first, the subjective acquisition of knowledge; in the second, product and interpretation of knowledge through subjective cultural representation, in the form of values, traditions and beliefs; and in the third, imposition by a dominant and forceful culture's masking presentation of the objectivity of knowledge's acquisition, concealing the reality, that it is subjective. This reveals the subjectivity of knowledge's acquisition to be manifested through the culturally ideological influences of imperialism and relativism.

Epistemology's Role

Defining knowledge in any discourse or discipline including human rights is problematic: "…to think of knowledge which presents a "problem" and about which we ought to have a "theory" is a product of viewing knowledge as an assemblage of representations…".[132] The problem of knowledge and its meaning[133] finds genesis as early as the 5th Century BC, notably in the work of Plato and Aristotle. The Greek Sophists questioned whether knowledge was subjective or objective. Gorgias maintained that nothing actually exists, that if it did so, it could not be known or communicated. By contrast, Protagoras claimed: "that no persons opinions can be said to be more correct than another's, because each is the sole judge of his or her own experience."[134]

Plato, following the teachings of Socrates countered the Sophists profound pessimism, claiming the world to exist upon a foundation "of unchanging and invisible forms"[135] through which knowledge would be revealed. Belief in the discovery of unchanging and invisible forms of knowledge, gave support to an objective body of reality, associated to the physical material world. Aristotle part resolved the argument between objectivity and subjectivity, contending that whilst the acquisition of knowledge was derived from experience, objectivity could be claimed, for experience acts as the receptor of the physical material world, to make visible unchanging forms.

Sympathetic to them, Immanuel Kant[136] recognised the ancient philosophers argument by scientifically differentiating between modes of expression, dividing the two schools of thought into either analytical (subjective) or synthetic (objective) propositions,[137] empirical or a priori. Empirical depends entirely on sense perception or the personal thoughts and feelings of an individual. Conversely, a priori did not depend upon sense perception; the objects of the material world are fundamentally unknowable, when devoid of reason, however, when sensations and ultimately reason are formed, they merely serve as the raw material. He claimed objects themselves had no existence; space and time exist only as part of the mind, as intuitions by which perceptions are measured and judged, a subjective truth, hence Kant's rationalization of objectivity emanating from the subjective:

> "Practical principles are propositions that contain a general determination of the will, having under it several practical rules. They are subjective, or maxims, when the condition is regarded by the subject as holding only for his will; but they are objective, or practical laws, when the condition is cognised as objective, that is, as holding for the will of every rational being."[138]

His apparent reconciliation of two seemingly opposing views lead Richard Rorty[139] to summarise how Kant was able to conclude this: "Kant put philosophy 'on the secure path of science' by putting outer space inside inner space...and then claiming Cartesian certainty about the inner for the laws of what had previously been thought to be outer..."[140] Despite his belief of universal laws originating from subjectivity, Kant forewarned the risk of accepting subjectivity as if it were a universal law. He foresaw subjects acquiring possession of their very own hypothesis of universal laws and the imminence of ensuing conflict, as a consequence of conceptual disagreement with other subjects:

> "For whereas elsewhere a universal law of nature makes everything harmonious here, if one wanted to give the maxim the universality of law, the most extreme opposite of harmony would follow, the worst conflict and the complete annihilation of the maxim itself and its purpose."[141]

Kant's Subjective "Moral Law"

Kant maintained, if an individual's analysis is not accepted universally then it remains the moral position of the individual, deficient in legality, hence drawing a clear distinction between law and morality:

> "If the determination of the will takes place conformably with the moral law but only by means of a feeling, of whatever kind

that has to be presupposed in order for the law to become a sufficient determining ground of the will, so that the action is not done for the sake of the law then the action will contain legality…"[142]

In revealing: "…the deliberate and mutual violation of man's most sacred rights",[143] Kant's recognition of man's possession of hallowed rights, is unique for the period in which he wrote and places him among modern sponsors of human rights, for man's most sacred rights are his human rights. More astounding, is his appreciation of the subjection of these rights to abuse, describing the torrent of torment as "deliberate and mutual violation". In proposing protection of these rights, Kant tenders the conception of evolving universal rights, through a universal medium:" is a [state] of international right (analogous to the civil or national rights of individual men) based on public laws backed by force and submitted to every nation."[144] Qualifying his observation, Kant suggested the utopian vision to be surmountable, however deficient in durability: "For an enduring universal peace brought about by a so called balance of power in Europe is a mere figment of imagination."[145]

In drawing the direct correlation between the ultimate ambition of man to progress and how he may do so by exercising morality and law, Kant's depressive vision offers a hopeful solution, as he provides advancement through the evolving of cultures:" since the human race's natural end is to make steady cultural progress, its moral end is to be conceived as progressing toward the better…"[146] and thus the embedded concentration, in his later works,[147] of the relationship between philosophy and law. The submission of an ethical system established on the conviction that reason is the final authority for morality, alleges actions of any sort must be undertaken from a sense of duty dictated by reason; on the contrary no action performed for expediency, or solely in obedience to law or custom can be regarded as moral. In an application of his scientific method, Kant is able to reconcile morality and law with the hypothetical imperative, dictating a given course of action to reach a specific end; and the categorical imperative, determining a course of action that must be followed because of its rightness and necessity. His support of the categorical imperative as the basis of morality allows Kant to bridge the divide between morality and law, declaring one to be a logical consequence to the other, for if an action must be followed because it is right and necessary, it is moral, subsequently morality develops into a natural law: "Act as if the maxim of your action were to become through your will a general natural law."[148] This I term Kant's "Moral Law". His ethical ideas were a logical outcome of his belief in the fundamental freedom of the individual. He did not regard this freedom as the lawless freedom of anarchy, but rather as the freedom of self-government, the autonomy to obey consciously the laws of the universe as revealed by reason. He supposed that the welfare of each individual should properly be regarded as an end in itself and that the world must advance toward an ideal society in which reason would:

> "Bind every law giver to make his laws in such a way that they could have sprung from the united will of an entire people and to regard every subject, in so far as he wishes to be a citizen, on the basis of whether he has conformed to that will."[149]

Kant ventured the notion in the establishment of a world federation of republican states,[150] the formation of universal ideals, agreed upon by and applicable to mankind as a whole.

Rorty's Objectivity

In rotating the ancient argument over the objectivity or subjectivity of knowledge, Rorty said:

> "It is pictures rather than propositions, metaphors rather than statements, which determine most of our philosophical convictions. The picture which holds traditional philosophy captive is that of the mind as a great mirror, containing various representations...some accurate, some not...and capable of being studied by pure, non empirical methods. Without the notion of the mind as a mirror, the notion of knowledge as accuracy of representation would not have suggested itself. Without this latter notion, the strategy common to Descartes

and Kant...getting more accurate representations by inspecting, repairing and polishing the mirror, so to speak would not have made sense..."[151]

His hypothesis that each observes the world through differing and varying representations is superficially reflective of a subjective inspection of knowledge; how a subject holds true their interpretation of knowledge, where another considers it false. Rorty acknowledges his metaphorical analogy of the mirror to be consistent with entrenched and active beliefs:

"I have been speaking as if the familiar oppositions between sense and intellect, confused and clear ideas, etc...were all parts of a modern artefact called 'theory of knowledge.' But even, if one grants that the philosophical sense of experience is a modern artefact, surely the Greek distinction between sense and intellect was a genuine discovery, as much a discovery as that of the rigorous provability of geometrical truth? And surely Kant was asking a good question when asked how necessary truth was possible?"[152]

Rorty is compelling, for he falsely supports subjectivity of knowledge through a differing interpretation of the mirror. He betrays the ancient and eighteenth century philosophers, by observing their values to be only of historical importance and of no relevance in the field of modern analytic thought. His true purpose is to deconstruct subjective concepts so that a "philosophy without mirrors"[153] may emerge.[154] He disregards the Kantian philosophy, of knowledge emanating from the subjective; he proffers the objectivity of knowledge and the invisible forms. Challenging the ancients, he argues thus:

"The difficulty stems from a notion shared by Platonists, Kantians and positivists: that man has an essence-namely, to discover essences. The notion that our chief task is to mirror accurately, in our own Glassy Essence, the universe around us is the complement of the notion, common to Democritus and

Descartes, that the universe is made up of very simple, clearly and distinctly knowable things, knowledge of whose essences provides the master-vocabulary which permits commensuration of all discourses."[155]

It is the essence to which he protests: "...we cannot take the notion of 'essence' seriously, nor the notion of man's task as the accurate representation of essences."[156]

Rejecting essence results in unrestricted objective exploration through scientific and analytic examination, by employing established scientific methods: psychophysiology and the sociology of knowledge:[157]

> "...By proclaiming that we have no essence, it permits us to see the descriptions of ourselves we find in one of the Naturwissenschaften as on a par with various alternative descriptions offered by poets, novelists, depth psychologists, sculptors, anthropologists and mystics."[158]

Rorty is of the conviction that an objective educative interrogation by the natural sciences of the "invisible forms" will ultimately guide man to their visibility:

> "The natural sciences, by themselves, leave us convinced that we know both what we are and what we can be...for 'objectivity' is the attempt to prevent education from being reduced to instruction the results of normal inquiry."[159]

In assaulting the subjective argument Rorty exploits truth as a weapon to destroy subjectivity, asserting the word to possess objectivity. He claims truth to sustain the same meaning for everyone and reveals this through analytical and scientific application, by interrogating everything in an impartial and detached manner. Applying this approach, Rorty enunciates that any meaning of any word or phrase, including the meaning of knowledge, will be true in the objective and hold the same meaning for everyone: "The term 'true'...means the same in all cultures, just as equally flexible terms like 'here', 'there', 'good', 'bad', 'you' and 'me' mean the same in all cultures."[160] His support of objectivity does not come without concession, for he acknowledges objectivity to be equally countered by subjectivity: "...to place 'objectivity', rationality, and normal inquiry within the larger picture...is often countered by the 'positivist' attempt to distinguish learning facts from acquiring values."[161] Similarly, Rorty confesses the ability of subjects to reveal truth through divergent and differing analysis, convinced, however, each will discover the same truth:

> "The identity of meaning is, of course, compatible with diversity of reference, and with diversity of procedures for assigning the term. The use and the meaning of the term 'true' remains the same even after diverse interrogative procedure."[162]

The analogy is not disparate, for example, of modern discoveries in astronomical science. Astronomers, as subjects, may utilize opposing techniques amongst themselves, to acquire knowledge of universal objects and thus determine the truth of the universe. The contrasting procedures of telescopy, the revealing of the universe by magnified sight and spectroscopy, through light, will with complete certainty permit the astronomers to acquire knowledge of the same universal objects, consequently providing the same truths.

William James[163] and Donald Davison[164] conclude the pursuit of knowledge as a "hopeless quest"[165] representative of Gorgias, where nothing actually exists and the revelation of truth through the acquisition of knowledge are not a reason or part of anything: "Davidson does not want to see truth identified with anything. He also does not want to view sentences as 'made true' by anything- neither knowers and or speakers on the one hand nor 'the world' on the other."[166] Rejecting both Kant's subjective knowers and speakers and Rorty's invisible forms, Davidson surrenders to Gorgias' void of nothingness. Independently, Michael Foucault believes the weapon of truth to be a device to brandish power: "truth is always an instrument of power"[167] strength is gained and sustained by knowledge's subjective acquisition and the consequent discovery of subjective truths, power dictates the compounding of subjective truths, to an elevation of the imposition of ideology:

"Ideology is not exclusive of scientificity. Few discourses have given so much place to ideology as clinical discourse or that of political economy: this is not a sufficiently good reason to treat the totality of their statements as being undermined by error, contradiction and a lack of objectivity."[168]

In supporting the proponents of subjectivity, Heisenberg declares truth to be manufactured by the subjectivity of the investigator acquiring knowledge. Discarding the objectivity of the laws of nature he proffers the subjectivity of laws created by men for men: "Since the measuring device has been constructed by the observer... we have to remember that what we observe is not nature in itself but nature exposed to our method of questioning." [169]

Law's Epistemology

Echoing the Kantian subjective concept of knowledge and rejecting Rorty's objectivity, the jurist Oliver Wendell Holmes referred its application to law, thus: "The common law is not a brooding omnipresence in the sky but the articulate voice of some sovereign or quasi sovereign that can be identified..."[170] I do not disclaim Rorty's objectivity, for I believe his argument has substance when the acquiring of knowledge is disconnected and unconcerned with the humanities. Scientific and analytical processes, I consider must be confined to the sciences alone and new methodologies must be created in the analysis of man's inter relations with his fellow man. The maxim: "no one should be above the law",[171] must still be guarded as a sacred hypothesis. Yet, in order to possess universal acceptance the law will always emanate in the first instance, as moral law, in the mind of a person, who must secure support from other subjects whom collectively attempt to elevate it to legality. For example, in Parliament, either the Government, opposition, or private members acting in support of pressure groups, daily collectively present bills to the House; propositions that originated in the mind of a person, a subject. Their presentation before the House exhibits the ability of the subject to have attained collective support amongst other subjects; if successful, the House pass the bill as an Act and the subject's moral law promotes to legality and becomes universally accepted. Clearly, law is not a discipline of the sciences, for it does not exist as a law of nature and therefore cannot be subjected to scientific analysis. I propose a different methodology to analysing the acquisition of knowledge in law, for it is attained in the inter relations of man with his fellow man. I suggest cultural analysis to be the correct method of examination, as man as a subject, is part of a body of subjects, whom hold similar values, traditions and beliefs, a trinity that culture is built upon.

Culture

In reasoning culture, it is unsurprising to discover, it possesses varying contextual connotations, however I proffer, for the context to which this thesis refers an accepted contemporary cross cultural definition. Culture is:

> "the set of distinctive spiritual, material, intellectual and emotional features of society or a social group, and that it encompasses, in addition to art and literature, lifestyles, ways of living together, value systems, traditions and beliefs."[172]

I shall now settle culture with Kant's subjective acquisition of knowledge and it is practical I repeat some propositions made earlier, to attest the causal association between them. Kant, confirmed knowledge to be acquired by a subject, through his reasoning, the moral law of that individual. Acceptance of it by other subjects elevates his knowledge, to an objective paradigm, as their knowledge, and thus knowledge's progress. Its growth, Kant affirms, derives from culture, as knowledge is acquired and cultivated by subjects; thus a "steady cultural progress" develops. The transition of a subject's moral law to legality transpires upon its recognition and approval by many other subjects, within that culture. The ability of subjects to agree upon a set of "value systems, traditions and beliefs" produces a commonality and communality amongst this set of subjects, a clear identity of their cultural grouping. I term this set of subjects, the cultural class. A subject acquiring knowledge will achieve acceptance of his truth provided he sustains recognition by his cultural class; an objective truth, within a cultural class, yet a subjective one in relation to other cultural classes.

In introducing Foucault's, "truth [as an] instrument of power" and his belief in the elevation of the subjective acquisition of knowledge to ideology, I now develop two hypothesis of choice, open to a cultural class. In the first, in the discovery of its truth a cultural class may suppress itself from using truth as an instrument of power. The class may determine that it is best to mutually accept to co exist with a diversity of truths, amongst other cultural classes. It may seek to channel its newly acquired power to discover ways and means to find common ground with other cultural classes and where such is found, mutually agree to elevate these values from their relativist subjectivity to a collective objectivity. This is the path of cultural relativism. In the second, a cultural class may use their truths as an instrument of power through ideology to enforce other cultural classes to discard their truths. By forcefully assimilating other cultural classes into their ideology, the cultural class attains objectivity of their truth, which otherwise would have remained subjective. This is the path of cultural imperialism.

Human Rights

In this section I aim to apply practically the theoretical model constructed in the previous pages by interrogating human rights as knowledge. Firstly, I examine its definition and show how the diversity amongst cultural classes contributes to the difficulty of a truly objective definition. Secondly, I volunteer reasoning to why there is difficulty in attaining objectivity of definition, claiming there to be a conglomeration of several constituents mediating human rights discourse, of which I term cultural principles. Thirdly, I provide evidence of the constituents working solely or in tandem to produce diverse definitions of human rights. Lastly I establish the effect of the constituents on cultural imperialism and how they may forcefully raise a cultural classes subjective view of human rights to an objective paradigm.

An Examination of a Definition for Human Rights and the Problems in the Search for Objective Meaning

"Cultures manifest so wide and diverse a range of preferences, morality, motivations, and evaluations that no human rights principles can be said to be self evident and recognised at all times and all places."[173]

Jerome Shestack is exactly right in making this observation, for it is the constant of culture itself, which presents the problematic of an objective definition of human rights. The phrase "Human Rights" holds many different meanings for many different cultural classes and it is this subjectivity, which makes finding an objective definition, so elusive, for it is the trinity of value systems, traditions and beliefs within the class which act as the expressions of knowledge and as a consequence human rights will be discussed within any of the frames of reference, pertaining to the trinity. Such frames of reference include the belief and tradition of religion, a belief in the existence of a creator and traditionalised through preaching and prayer. Another is the value system of law, created from within a cultural class' ethics and morals and traditionalised in the exercise of the law through, its executive, legislative and judiciary. Rosenbaum[174] recognised the frames of reference by creating specific principles to support human rights. It is these principles, which I claim, give reasoning to the difficulty in defining human rights objectively.

Rosenbaum's Principles, as Reasoning for the Problems in Objective Definition. The Development of a "Cultural Principle"

Rosenbaum claims there to be four general principles, which support human rights. The Ethical principle functions on the premise that: human rights are mans moral obligations towards his fellow man; the bond between morality and human rights is so intertwined that nothing can actually separate them.[175] The Theological principle relates human rights with a religious context, rights that are conferred upon man by God.[176] The Historical principle operates on the evolving of the human mind. As mans mind becomes more and more aware of the world around him over time, so his sense for human rights naturally and reciprocally evolves.[177] The Political principle works on the premise that human rights is but one component of a political ideal such as democracy and that in a true democracy, human rights flourishes alongside it.[178] I do not discount with lesser importance the existence of the four main principles, but see them more as derivatives emanating from a much higher principle, which I shall name the cultural principle. It is an umbrella principle which unifies common elements co existing within a cultural class, for each class has at its core the fundamental principles of morals (of which laws may evolve), religion, politics all of which historically have emanated from the state of mind of an individual or group of individuals within that cultural class. The cultural principle can thus be described as the value systems, traditions and beliefs of a cultural class, personified through its moral/legal, religious, political and historical structures.

The problem in defining human rights is, therefore, reasoned, as it is the emphasis to which a cultural class places upon certain constituents, within the cultural principle that determines a cultural classes definition of human rights. These constituents, either works solely or in tandem, to offer differing interpretations of human rights.

Evidence of Rosenbaum's Principles Producing Diverse Definitions of Human Rights. Cultural Relativism in Action

I shall now give two examples of the constituents producing diverse definitions of human rights. In the first instant, I provide an example of constituents working in tandem and in the second, I offer the role of a singular constituent, in the production of a completely different definition of human rights.

Ethical, Theological, Political and Historical – Principles in Tandem

The moulding of a definition using all four constituents of the cultural principle can be seen within western culture, for it is historically sprung from the geographical area of Western Europe, developed by the ethical constituent of Greek philosophy and Roman law, and the theological constituent of the Judaeo Christian tradition and lastly the political constituent of Humanism of the Reformation and the Age of Reason.[179] The current Parliamentary democracies of Western Europe and the United States are the inheritors of this tradition. These Western cultures have either carried these values to other parts of the world, through colonization and empire, or have allowed their cultural philosophy on human rights to be assimilated by other cultures in whole or in part. The modern Western approach to human rights can be found as early as the 18th Century, more particularly France in 1879, where it had been declared:

> "The aim of all political association is the conservation of the natural and inalienable rights of man. These rights are: Liberty, Property, Security, and Resistance to oppression."[180]

It is of note that the declaration above, does not go onto discuss why these rights are "natural" or "inalienable", indeed no explanation is offered, the authors of the declaration believing in the presumption that the explanation of such terms were already obvious, given that the presumption was already imbedded in western culture, through philosophical and religious teaching. The doctrine of natural law had already been established at this time, as being laws of nature or laws of God above and beyond positive law created by Man. Clearly a direct throw back to western cultures foundations in Greek philosophy and the concepts of Plato and Socrates that these natural and inalienable rights were "unchanging and invisible forms".

The French Declaration of the Rights of Man and the Citizen 1789, proclaimed a number of entitlements which are now generally called civil and political rights: the basic principle that all men are born and remain free and equal in their rights; also particular rights, including equality before the law, freedom from arrest except in conformity with the law, the presumption of innocence, protection against retroactivity of the law, freedom of opinion, freedom of expression, and the well know definition of liberty as freedom to do anything which is not harmful to others. The Magna Carta of 1215, in England guaranteed to the citizen the freedom from imprisonment or from dispossession of his property and freedom from prosecution or exile: "unless by the lawful judgement of his peers or by the law of the land." It also included a primitive formulation of the right to fair trial: "To none will we sell, deny or delay right of justice." Human rights in England predate the French Declaration As examples we need not look further than one hundred years prior to the French Declaration, with an examination of the Habeas Corpus Acts and the Bill of Rights 1689. These assured the supremacy of Parliament, the right to free elections, freedom of speech, the right to bail, freedom from cruel and unusual punishments and the right to trial by jury. The independence of the judiciary and the freedom of the press were established thereafter.

The works of Montesquieu,[181] Voltaire and Jean Jacques Rousseau,[182] in Paris, during the 18th century, did much to advance the western concept of human rights. The western philosophy that emerged was itself built upon the work of the English philosopher, John Locke[183] whom, a century earlier and following the "Glorious Revolution" of 1688, had advocated that the rights of man emanated from "...the state of nature, before humankind entered civil society..."[184] It is of interest to note the western concept ignores the Kantian philosophy advocated at the time, that such rights emerge from the subjective of man himself, but more so, in the Rorty sense, that these rights were a part of the very fabric, of man's surroundings, that they existed in the natural world, that they were there waiting to be discovered by him. The works of these new wave philosophers sparked the imagination within France and the fledgling United States of America, in the 18th and 19th Century, no more so inspired was Thomas Jefferson, who wrote: "... free people claiming their rights as derived from the laws of nature and not as the gift of their Chief Magistrate…"[185] Later to be echoed in the United States of America Declaration of Independence:[186]

> " We hold these truths to be self evident, that all men are created equal, that they are endowed by their Creator with certain unalienable rights, that among these are Life, Liberty and the pursuit of happiness."[187]

Thus the wave of new found freedom of man spread the western world, with similar declarations, in particular the Marquis de Lafayette proclaiming in the French Declaration of the Rights of Man and the Citizen:[188] "…men are born and remain free and equal in rights…"[189] Having established in its western manifestation that man had "rights", its philosophers and writers began to establish the nature of these "rights". Hohfeld[190] saw such as falling into four broad categories:

> "…a claim right, where one person asserts he has a claim on another; a liberty right, which authorises a person to do as he pleases…a power, by which a person is enabled or empowered… and an immunity, which protects a person from the power of another."[191]

Dworkin[192] saw these rights as reciprocal, so for example where a claim right to privacy existed, others would be also duty bound to honour such a right. He saw such rights as fundamental to the social and economic well being of the state, as mechanisms for improving the moral and legal standing of it.[193] Others, however, have seen the western concept of human rights not to be so advantageous, contemporaries, such as Nozick[194] and Raz[195] see such "rights" as hindrance and conversely are of the view, that whilst "…every individual has exclusive rights in himself"[196] no person should "violate the rights of others",[197] a view to reflect that no person has the right to impose human rights, on others.

The Theological Principle – Acting on its own

I now provide two examples where the constituent of theology has acted solely upon its own to develop a completely different definition of human rights. In the first, I examine the influence of the theology of Hinduism and in the second Islam. Hinduism does not see human rights as rights per se, but more so duties, handed down by the ultimate creator to individuals, whom themselves form a miniscule part of the constituents of the universe and its reality. For, Hindu's see their human rights, in the sense of survival. It is their function in the scheme of the universe, which is paramount, their lokasamgraha, and their right to exist in a place preordained, by the constant cycle of life, death and reincarnation. Their rights as human beings are placed in the hierarchical ladder that is the caste system, where each caste from the highest to the lowest are provided with duties to perform in this life and into the next, until the individual has achieved the right to complete freedom and eternal enlightenment.[198] This concept has no parallel with the western ideal of human rights, other than the commonality of the theological principle of an ultimate creator granting rights to man. The western analogy sees such rights as gifts from the creator, given freely; the Hindu concept conversely sees such as prizes that must be won and are only rewarded through complete fulfilment of the duties and life challenges set by the creator.

Islam's definition of human rights is based on its followers holding true to the word of Islam, the Qur'an and the Shari 'a law that emanates from it. A Muslim sees rights, much in the same way, as a Hindu, as a series of duties to the creator, in order to attain the higher freedom of universal enlightenment, at death. The Shari 'a is not considered a strict codified law, with literal interpretation, notwithstanding, the flexibility of its nature, it has very much over time, left disagreement and conflict, even amongst its own, Muslim followers. However, there are instances where strict literal interpretation can and will only be tolerated, if such direct conflict arises with western concepts of human rights. For example, the Shari 'a law of apostasy, the denunciation of the Muslim religion, by a Muslim directly repudiating the Islamic faith.[199] Clearly, a law, which conflicts with the human right for the freedom of religion. The publication of Satanic Verses by Salman Rushdie and the subsequent edict by Imam Khomeini of Iran, for his sentence to death, in absentia, without charge or trial during the 1980's, demonstrates further how the western concept of the human right to free speech, can be flagrantly flouted by Shari 'a law. The Shari 'a law of quawama,[200] the ownership of man over woman restricts the rights of women, such human rights which under a western view would be readily given; the right to vote, the right to free speech, are examples of just some of these. To say that Shari 'a law is totally in direct conflict with the western concept of human rights, is plainly not true, for in a number of verses, within the Qur'an there are references to "Human Kind, the children of Adam",[201] denoting the connotation that reference is made to all of humanity, irrespective, of race, colour, creed or sex. If compromise were have to be reached in establishing common ground between different concepts of human rights, in this instance between the western and Muslim concepts then I believe it is within the Shari 'a law first, this should be achieved, so as not to cause offence to disregard and disrespect an ever growing faith. To exploit areas of the Qur'an, which lend verse to commonality with western concepts, would reconcile mutually any differences in their relativist structures.

The Effect of Rosenbaum's Principles on Cultural Imperialism's Influence of Human Rights Definition

I have briefly highlighted the expanse of the gulf that lies between certain relativist hypothesis towards human rights and demonstrated why such would reveal discourse within it. I shall now examine in the final part of this chapter, how the constituents the cultural principle or Rosenbaum's principles have affected cultural imperialism and how that has impacted upon human rights and its elevation to an apparent universal standard.

Cultural imperialism's impact upon human rights is much dependent upon a cultural classes bargaining power, amongst other cultures. Other cultures are compelled to accept apparent universal standards because they are pressured to do so by their more powerful cultural counterparts, such great cultural powers that in this sense exercise the externalisation of their ideology. All cultures seek to maintain their uniqueness, wherever possible, however, they are equally sceptical of the power that other cultures may or could impose upon them. One culture that is all powerful, cannot alone impose its ideology upon all other cultures, but must be supported in its hegemonic view, if a binding human rights regime is to be established, as holding an apparent objective standard. Therefore, a group of great cultural powers, with not dissimilar value systems, beliefs and traditions, exercising the same constituents of the cultural principle, shall hold greater weight, for they may collectively coerce or induce less powerful cultures to accept, or adjust to their view of human rights standards. This view is supported by the history within western culture:

> "...much of the explanation for the Inter American human rights regime...lies in power, particularly the dominant power of the United States...it exercised its hegemonic power to ensure its creation and support its operations."[202]

In collating a collective alliance with other similar cultures, the United States has also had success: "Like some earlier great powers, the United States can identify the presumed duty of the rich and powerful to help others with their own beliefs...England claimed to bear the white man' burden; France had its mission civilisatrice...for countries at the top, this is predictable behaviour."[203] Hence, cultures accept binding international human rights norms, because they are swayed by an overpowering ideological power, of which the United States, since the Second World War, represents: "The seemingly inescapable ideological appeal of human rights in the post world war is an important element in the rise of international human rights regimes."[204] Modern cultural imperialism, hence finds its genesis with the establishment of American cultural values, shortly after the cessation of the Second World War, collectively assimilated through similar cultures: the United Kingdom and France and then imposed upon other cultures by persuasion, coercion, or force, to allow, in the instance of human rights, it to be elevated to an acceptable universal standard. What have been the vehicles used by powerful ideological cultures, to persuade lesser cultures to come within the fold of their vision of human rights? The answer to this question lies in the construction of the apparently universally acceptable institutions and their dispensation of apparently universal instruments, which claimed to speak the law for all of humanity.

Human Rights Institutions and Instruments

To continue to develop the argument that the declaration of human rights, as an objective enterprise is in reality predicated on subjective norms, I shall investigate the development of "global" institutions, and how they endeavour to exercise their view of human rights, through the consequent creation of instruments, in the form of apparent universal declarations or agreements, to which all cultures agree to comply. I shall briefly outline, historically, how institutions such as the United Nations and the International Military Tribunal's of Nuremberg and Tokyo, were used to exercise the western and culturally imperialistic standard of human rights justice and how certain declaratory instruments were created by western cultural powers alone.

Cultural Imperialism's Influence on the Founding of Human Rights Institutions and Instruments

I propose that the creation of apparent global institutions were subjectively constructed, in that, they were formed, from the background of one dominant cultural class and at their outset these institutions were able to create apparent international legal agreements, in the form of declaratory instruments, which were not in reality, universal, but reflected their subjective view. I choose below examples of this very process.

The Subjectivity of Opinio Juris

One basis for international law is the doctrine of opinio juris. The maxim states that:

> "...customary international law results from (a) the uniform
> and consistent conduct of States, undertaken with (b) the

conscious conviction on the part of States that they are acting in conformity with law, or that they were required so to act by law."[205]

In itself, it is easy to interpret the rhetoric of the doctrine to be a reflection of the collectiveness of States, mutually agreeing and accepting international customary rules, whilst maintaining the exclusivity of their own relative backgrounds. Mutual agreement and acceptance, derives the notion that States have consented, to conform to international law and the introduction of the concept of consent has been referred to as the "postponement" theory.[206] The theory suggests, that a State may of its own and subjective accord, commence a practice, for which it alone conducts. At that moment in time, it is not considered to be opinio juris. It only so becomes, should that State be able to negotiate the consent of other States such that the rule of law has general applicability to all States. The question then arises as to how that individual State, sets about obtaining consent from other States, more importantly how that State is able to convince other States of the general relevance of its own subjective belief and values, for which the practice reflects. As I shall set out below, the persuasion to obtain apparent consent, is founded on the premise that a State which unilaterally establishes a practice, is one which has capacity to do so, for it is culturally dominant, over others. It has the ability to coerce other States, of less stature, into conforming, thereby elevating the practice to a universally accepted and objective paradigm. This method of obtaining apparent consent, has been the procedure employed by western culture, to establish its' exercising of human rights practices. "To objectify a rule",[207] for example, human rights, lessens the strength of any opposing individual state to claim such human rights principles are wrong. The State, whom invented the practice, is in a much stronger position, to claim its universality despite its previous subjectivity. I shall now show below by using the example of the United Nations creation, how western culture had employed this method to coerce consent from other States, to establish, itself, its human rights practices and the establishment of apparent universal declaratory instruments.

The United Nations Creation – Western Culture's Influence?

The preamble of the United Nations Charter[208] states:

> "We the peoples of the United Nations determined to save succeeding generations from the scourge of war, which twice in our life time has brought untold sorrow to mankind, and to reaffirm faith in fundamental human rights, in the dignity and worth of the human person, in the equal rights of men and women and of nations large and small..."[209]

This represents a clear statement of universal intention by all member states, to agree a universal set of standards and norms to ensure the cessation of hostilities and the promotion of universal human rights. It is important to investigate the originators of these utopian and high ideals.

The creation of the "United Nations"[210] was as a consequence of proposals initially made by the United Kingdom and the United States, the new ascending cultural powers, during the Second World War; who realised the need to convince other nations of their culturally driven concepts. This was achieved at Dumbarton Oaks, USA between August and October 1944.[211] In working upon their proposals with China, the Soviet Union and France, the United States and the United Kingdom were able to move forward with implementation of their concepts, thereby elevating their subjective cultural principles to an apparent objective and universal standard.

The technique employed by the United States and the United Kingdom remains significant, for it has acted as the blueprint for the imposition of dominant western cultural value systems, traditions and beliefs, upon the rest of humanity. The United States has never shied from proclaiming that their cultural values must be dominant and accepted by other cultures; since it is based upon the premise that their value systems, traditions and beliefs, are correct for all mankind. The oratory of United States President's, pre and post United Nations formation, evidentially supports this:

"Nothing is more essential to the future peace of the world than continued cooperation of the nations which had to muster the force necessary to defeat the conspiracy of the Axis powers to dominate the world…These great states have a special responsibility to enforce the peace."[212]

"We [the United States] recognize and accept our own deep involvement in the destiny of men everywhere."[213]

At formation, the United Nations comprised only fifty-eight member states out of a possible one hundred and eighty.[214] The majority of members were closely affiliated because of colonial ties with culturally imperial powers, principally in Europe and hence the reality that these member states had little say in their own cultural destiny, because of the dominance of and assimilation by western culture, over them. No Far East Asian, Arab or African states, other than western culturally influenced South Africa, Syria and Saudi Arabia were represented at the United Nations.[215] United Nation membership did change slowly over time, notwithstanding western culture's continued influence and dominance of the United Nations.

The creation, by a dominant western cultural class, of the United Nations laid the burden of responsibility in this class to ensure peace, security and human rights over other cultures, the benefit being that their beliefs, traditions and value systems (disseminated through their cultural principle) would become the dominant and universal norm. Further, ultimately, it gave the western cultural class the opportunity to establish other apparent universal institutions, namely the supposed international tribunals to try Nazi and Japanese war criminals, (the International Military Tribunals for Nuremberg and Tokyo) when the true reality was that they were little more than a reflection of western cultural construct and reminiscent of institutional structures within dominant western culture.

Nuremberg and Tokyo – Western Cultures Judicial Force?

To demonstrate the façade of these universal institutions, I shall briefly consider the historical background from which such tribunals were established, for the concept of trial by tribunal was not new.

During the 19th century, Europe was the central hub of modernity, wealth and power and it very much saw itself as the international community, for it regarded other cultures that bordered its boundaries and beyond, to be backward and subject to their imperialist exploitation, through colonialism. Within the western cultural base of Europe, there began a closer co-operation between nation states. Their illusion that they solely occupied the mantle of the international community is evidenced by the rhetoric of the time. By example, the Declaration of Vienna 1815, proclaimed the defeated Napoleon as an "International Outlaw".[216] It is questionable if Asian or African cultures were aware of the identity of Napoleon. Academics, generally, have recognised Europe's psychological mindset, that international law's origins were subjectively based:

> "Savigny recognised a community of race and religion at least in Europe, which he found to be the basis of International Law."[217]

Western culture's illusion, continued into the early 20th century. The United Kingdom, with the aid of the United States, the principle victors of World War I sought, in 1919, to bring Kaiser Wilhelm II to justice, for his part in the atrocities committed by his nation. The then United States President, Woodrow Wilson feared that by doing so, would only bring considerable unrest and play into the hands of the new communist government of Russia. He expressly sated this fear: "Had you rather have the Kaiser or the Bolsheviks?" The ally convened the "Commission of Responsibilities of the Authors of the War and the Enforcement of Penalties." or as it was to become known, in its shorter form: "The Commission of 15." Convening in Paris, its Chairman Robert Lansing, U.S. Secretary of State appointed fifteen apparently international lawyers, two from each of the five major allies and then one each from five lesser states, within the European geographical area. No international lawyers were appointed outside the European geographical area and the western cultural sphere, hence any from Africa or Asia, in particular. The very fact that it's Chairman, was the United States Secretary of State, made clear the direction of the Commission's agenda. The construct of the Commission demonstrates the ability of a culturally imperial power to maintain and externalise their subjective hegemonic view, by drawing upon the aid of other like-minded cultures, to legitimise and provide objective credence, to it. In this instance the justification to put on trial the Kaiser. The Commission released its "Majority Report", on 29th March 1919 and recommended, "...a High Tribunal composed of judges drawn from many nations..."[218] should be established to try former Heads of State. The report made direct reference for the need to place the Kaiser on trial. As justification for such action the Report said: "...the vindication of the principles of the laws and customs of war and the laws of humanity which have been violated would be incomplete if he were not brought to trial and if other offenders less highly placed were punished..."[219]

The Commission then turned its attention to considering the laws of humanity which [had] been violated. It categorised the new crimes, the first of which amounted to:

"Acts which provoked the world war and accompanied its inception...the invasion of Luxembourg and Belgium...The premeditation of a war of aggression, dissimulated under a peaceful pretence, then suddenly declared under false pretexts..."[220]

The second category concerned: "Violations of the laws and customs of war and the laws of humanity." Such violations disseminated into a further four categories:

"Outrages by enemy countries against civilians and soldiers, such outrages being committed in prison or forced labour camps, to which such camps comprised prisoners from several nations. The orders given by those in authority on the enemy side, not only at the battle front, but where such orders also affected conduct in general against the allied armies. Those in authority, from the highest ranking to the lowest, including the heads of State, whom had knowledge of the atrocities but failed to intervene or to take measures to prevent the atrocities or failed to put an end to the violations of the laws or customs of war. Any other offence the High Tribunal sought fit to try under its jurisdiction."[221]

The First World War, was fought on European soil, the nations and their cultural composition were predominantly western European, and it can be accepted that a high tribunal to try Heads of State within its western cultural base, may have been the proper and correct way, however, to legitimise it as one which reflects the norms of all humanity and the international community is not. Even to qualify the legitimacy of the tribunal in a western cultural domestic sense is problematic. Even within the geographical area of Western Europe and the United States, there are finer cultural differences. For, they differ in their components of cultural principle. By way of example, the ethical constituent of law in the United States and the United Kingdom differs from that of Germany and other continental states. The United States and the United Kingdom, find theirs based upon Anglo-Saxon, adversarial systems, whereas, Germany, for example, find theirs on a Continental, investigative system. Further, the political constituent, finds clear differences in that, there was a melee, at the time, of democracies, dictatorships and monarchical governments scattered all over western culture. However, the commonality of religious Christian belief strengthened the common theological bond they all possessed. These minute differences in component of cultural principle within western culture would prove to be a continuing dilemma, in the construct of International Military Tribunals, following the cessation of the Second World War.

Nuremberg- Imperialism within Cultural Relativism

The first so called international war crimes trials began in November 1945 in Nuremberg, Germany. At that time Nuremberg, was situated in the American zone of the post war divided Germany, a Bavarian city, which had lay at the heart of the early years of the Nazi movements' formation. The United States, France, Great Britain and the Soviet Union set up the apparently international Military Tribunal. Prosecutors from those four countries indicted a total of 22 Nazi German officials on three basic charges:

- Conspiring and ultimately launching an "aggressive war"
- Committing war crimes
- Committing "crimes against humanity."[222]

Also indicted were various German organisations and businesses that the Allies charged with aiding the Nazi war effort. Among the atrocities that the Nazis were responsible for the murder of six million Jews throughout Europe and the destruction of thousands of cities and towns. All those indicted pleaded not guilty. Some claimed that they were merely following orders when they helped oversee the transport and murder of Jews and other minorities. Some argued that the tribunal had no jurisdiction. The lead prosecutor, Robert Jackson, a U.S. Supreme Court judge, disagreed:

> "The wrongs which we seek to condemn and punish have been so calculated, so malignant and so devastating that civilization cannot tolerate their being ignored because it cannot survive their being repeated."[223]

Jackson and the other prosecutors focused primarily on charges of conspiracy, charges for which there was little legal precedent. They exhibited official German documents indicating that Nazi officials planned the extermination of Jews and other minorities. They also attempted to define the basic distinction between warfare as commonly conducted and atrocities that exceed "military necessity." The trials lasted 11 months. Of the 21 defendants in custody (one indicted Nazi, Martin Bormann, was indicted in absentia and was never found), a total of 11 were sentenced to death, three were acquitted and the rest received prison terms. Ten men were hanged in November 1946; one of those sentenced to death, Hermann Göring, committed suicide hours before his scheduled execution.

I shall now support my assertion that the Nuremberg Trials were not truly international, that their construct was not based on objective universal standards and did not exercise human rights for the whole of humanity; although one cannot disagree with the following statement, for the heinousness of the acts of those that committed them:

> "The German people may no longer remain passive before this tremendous amount of material. A judgement, which an International Military Tribunal has rendered on German territory, against Germans, should not leave any German unconcerned. Proceedings in which the law of nations is invoked for the first time in such a magnificent form against the abuse of power, should find the lively attention of the German people, even if Germany had not been directly involved." [224]

I have already alluded to the distinct lack of participation of other neutral nations, other than those directly and perceivably biased in the victors favour, during the war, in any aspect of the construction of the Tribunal, or within the conduct of the trials themselves. For, it was clear other cultural imprints were not evident in any aspect of the tribunal's design. However, what was clearly blatant for all to see was the western cultural face of the Tribunal. The eight judges that sat to hear the numerous trials did not sit under a universal flag, or in universal attire, to reflect the international rhetoric they had propounded. Judges sat behind their respective flags and in attire reflective of their traditional domestic judicial costume. Hence, the French sat in white jabots and the Soviets in brown military uniform.

It was argued, pre trial,[225] by German defence lawyers' that they were being asked to defend their clients under foreign legal principles. This had much to do with the adversarial Anglo-Saxon system, the foundation of English and United States law opposed to the inquisitive Continental style that the Germans were used to.[226] By way of example was the approach they gave to count one of the indictments against their clients, "The Common Plea of Conspiracy".[227] "Conspiracy" was not a term in Continental law, it developed from the Anglo- Saxon ethical principle of customary law, much like the phrase, "common plea". The purpose of allowing the indictment into the Tribunal's Charter was to ensure the widening of the class of people to be prosecuted, for the net would be spread to include those individuals whom were responsible as leaders in giving orders to those whom actually carried out the atrocities. This indictment was particularly useful, in that it allowed the prosecutors to place charges against the leaders of the Nazi movement whom had given the order to commit atrocity, but was not there at the time, the said atrocity was committed. In response to the abhorrence of the imposition of Anglo-Saxon law, one German lawyer wrote:

> "It must be constantly borne in mind that this is an American Court of Justice, applying the ancient and fundamental concepts of Anglo-Saxon jurisprudence."[228]

It had been very clear three years prior to Nuremberg that the United States at least wished to manoeuvre Tribunals the American way and the case of Ex Parte Quirin[229] is an example. This involved the trial of captured Nazi saboteurs, conducted before an American Military Commission, under judicial rules and procedures familiar only to the United States.

The Tokyo Trials – Cultural Imperialist Imposition

Western culture or predominantly the United States influence as the chief instrument in such trials orchestration progressed beyond Nuremberg, to Tokyo: "The Hollywood Premiere rolled into Tokyo, to look like a third string road company of the Nuremberg show."[230] Between its commencement in May 1946 and conclusion in November 1948, the tribunal tried over five thousand seven hundred Japanese at eight hundred and eighty court sessions, of which nine hundred and twenty were sentenced to death by execution.[231] In the trial of Prime Minister Tojo, there was no hiding the fact that the International Military Tribunal for Tokyo was not international in any sense of the word. It was conducted by the American Military, for their satisfaction and theirs alone: "I think we can say that to some extent the Tojo trial itself provided a wholesome example of a concept of Anglo-Saxon justice."[232] Further, confirmed by the Defendant himself: "In the last analysis, the trial was a political trial. It was only Victors Justice."[233]

I have made the point previously that even within a cultural class it is possible to receive differences in aspects of the cultural principle. I gave the example of how within Western culture; there may be variations of the ethical and political constituents, which in them can cause discourse within a culture, particularly in deciding to which legal structure, under its ethical constituent of cultural principle one chooses before trying subjects. Tokyo exemplifies and provides clear delineation of cultural class, for Japanese culture could not have been further than western culture, at the time of cessation of the Second World War. Granted, its history one hundred or so years prior to that War, reflected an ever growing encroachment of western influence with the surrender of some economic and legal rights to the United States during the Meiji period of 1868 to 1912. Such encroachment, impacted upon Japanese culture, in that the Emperor was forced to take central control and seize feudal lands from local nobles, subsequently leading to the demise of the Samurai, as protector and guardians of these lands. Having also fought wars successfully with China (1894-1895) and Russia (1904-5) Japan had endured troubled and turmoiled times as a consequence of other cultures influence upon it.[234] Despite this, Japan pre Second World War, still very much based itself upon its own value systems, traditions and beliefs and enhanced through its own unique constituents of cultural principle. "The Constitution of the Empire of Japan 1889" or "Tsuge – bumi"[235] supports this, for it placed all power before the Emperor of Japan. All constituents of cultural principle were to be dictated by the Emperor. For example: the religious, vested worship of the Emperor at Article 3; the political vested power in him also at Articles 4 and Articles 5 and 6 provided that he exercised all legislative and legal power, which he delegated through "a diet" and Privy Council.[236] The cessation of the Second World War naturally changed this and with predominantly American occupation of Japan, the assimilation of the western cultural principle commenced. The starting point was the radical change to the 1889 constitution, which took place shortly following the end of the war, adopted by Japan on the 3rd November 1946, effective 3rd May 1947.[237]

The relinquishment of absolute power from the Emperor was

fundamental to the new constitution, indeed its first chapter, Articles 1 to 8, deal directly in transfer of power from the Emperor to the people. He became simply a symbolic head of state[238] restricted to ceremonial functions only.[239] Democratisation, the political constituent within western culture, became a focus of the new constitution. The appointment of a Prime Minister and his cabinet, by the people through the western concept of one-man one vote, conferred for the first time electoral rights.[240] The western concept, for it was not one that previously existed in Japanese culture, of equal matrimonial rights[241] was introduced. The introduction of western judicial concepts, further lead credence to western assimilation, for the Latin phrase, terminology completely foreign to Japan, "Nulla Poena Sine Lege" prevented the trying twice of an individual, for the same crime.[242] Article 11 provided, for the first time, for fundamental human rights, although the constitution does not elaborate on the precise meaning of the term. One can assume, however, the introduction of it from western culture, would provide it with meaning attributable to those assimilating. The change in the feudal court system designed to western cultural specifications was also clear. The new Court system resembled American and European models; a Supreme Court at its head; followed by eight lower High Courts; fifty Family and fifty District Courts, followed lastly by four hundred and thirty eight summary Courts supports this view.[243]

Having demonstrated how western cultural imperialism was able to force its own subjective view of human rights through the establishment of the United Nations and the International Military Tribunals for Nuremberg and Tokyo, I shall now turn to the second method employed, the introduction of apparent declaratory instruments, through the United Nations, as demonstration of their ability to again raise their subjective view, to a universal and objective level. As example, I shall now examine the Universal Declaration of Human Rights 1948.

Universal Declaration of Human Rights 1948 – Truly Universally Accepted?

I have previously stated the founding members of the United Nations, to be few in number and to be unrepresentative of the whole of mankind, predominantly comprising western cultural states or those states that had been strongly assimilated with strong western cultural influence. I repeat this for reason, for it is important to assess the construction of the Universal Declaration of Human Rights 1948, in light of this background. Hence, it is unsurprising that the architects of this declaratory instrument were of western cultural origin: Eleanor Roosevelt of the United States, Rene Cassin of France and (despite his Lebanese birth), Charles Malik of Lebanon.[244] Even though the Declaration received adoration, as being: "…the International Magna Carta of all Mankind"[245] the reality is somewhat different. Not only did the instrument not have cross-cultural input by states outside the United Nations membership, those nations, which did vote for its inception and introduction, were influenced by imperial and colonial ties.[246] The writers of the instrument wrote from the perspective of the western cultural concept of human rights. It is its very elevation to an objective universal norm that set in stone the prevailing discourse:

> "…the Declaration…proceeded to work its subversive path through many rooted doctrines of international law, forever changing the discourse of international relations on issues vital to human decency and peace."[247]

Henry Steiner's referral to the instrument as subversive, is telling in itself, since, indoctrinating the western cultural subjective, into an apparent objective and universal norm had clearly been achieved:

> "To the relativist, these instruments and their pretension to universality may suggest primarily the arrogance of 'cultural imperialism' of the West, given the West's traditional urge. Moreover, the push to universalization of norms is said to destroy diversity of cultures and hence to amount to another part toward cultural homogenisation in the modern world…"[248]

The constituents of the cultural principle, that of politics and theology are considered by some to be the chief factors aiding elevation: "… given the West's traditional urge – expressed for example in political ideology and in religious faith- to view its own forms and beliefs as universal, and to attempt to universalise them…"[249]

A Broad "Membership" as a Palliative to Ethnocentrism

How then can we say that the United Nations has today moved away from its original western cultural construction? The answer lies in the growth of its membership. The acquisition of more member states, now standing at over one hundred and eighty, has allowed the opportunity for them to voice their view in determining the shaping and forming of the global cultural community. The diversity of cultures within the United Nations, unshackled by their own cultural independency and free over time from colonial and imperial ties, has allowed the United Nations to change its post second world war western cultural face. I shall now demonstrate how the United Nations has done this by examining the development of United Nations declaratory instruments, which from their obvious construct, provide evidence of the elevation of subjective views on human rights to the objective, through peaceful and mutually agreed means, by the majority of relativist cultures, under the globally cultural umbrella of the United Nations.

Redressing the Balance – The Influence of Cultural Relativism on Modern Human Rights Institutions and Instruments

I now aim to prove there has been a culturally ideological shift within human rights institutions, towards relativism and a corresponding shift within modern declaratory instruments. I shall do this by examining various declaratory instruments and further, I shall concentrate on two specific cases, before the International Criminal Tribunal for the former Yugoslavia and Rwanda that attest to this transfer.

Human Rights Declaratory Instruments Post 1948 – Relativist Influence?

I stated above that the membership of the United Nations has grown significantly since its inception and I shall now demonstrate how that membership, with its infiltration of cultural diversity, away from the 1948, western cultural norm, has had significant influence in the introduction an increase of human rights declaratory instruments, notwithstanding that such relativist influence has also changed the shape and form of the United Nations. I shall commence with the significance of the "Declaration on the Granting of Independence to Colonial Countries 1960", in itself not a human rights declaratory instrument, but one which reflects the pressure of relativist cultural states upon their introduction to the United Nations, to emboss their mark upon it.

Declaration on the Granting of Independence to Colonial Countries 1960

Not surprisingly, the increase in African cultural states membership of joining with the United Nations from 1960 onwards increased dramatically, such states being under the colonial influence of western cultural powers. I refer to Figure 3, above, with regard to UN membership, to demonstrate the rapid increase in the representation.

The period 1959 to 1961 reflects an exceptional increase in African cultural membership, an opportunity, therefore, to implore upon the United Nations, to recognise African culture's fundamental rights. The Declaration sought to recognise the African cultural states independence from that of its colonial, western cultural masters:

> "The subjection of peoples to alien subjugation, domination and exploitation constitutes a denial of fundamental human rights, is contrary to the Charter of the United Nations and is an impediment to the promotion of world peace and co-operation."[250]

The direct effect of this instrument was to immediately increase rapidly the independence to these cultural states:

"Immediate steps shall be taken, in Trust and Non-Self Governing Territories or all other territories which have not yet attained independence, to transfer all powers to the peoples of those territories, without any conditions or reservations, in accordance with their freely expressed will and desire, without any distinction as to race, creed or colour, in order to enable them to enjoy complete independence and freedom."[251]

This declaratory instrument serves to demonstrate how a grouping of culturally relativist states, (for they were so, since the composition of the United Nations had at this time grown to embrace the African cultural states) had mutually agreed, without force or imposition, to ensure that colonial, imperial domination would not directly affect and control their culture, a form of collective cultural relativism. This instrument had a rapid effect upon decolonisation and the assertion of cultural independence and the reinforcement of relativist culture over imperialist control, using the vehicle of a globally cultural institution, the United Nations, to affect its happening.

Further mutually agreed declaratory instruments were passed and these included: Declaration on the Rights of Persons Belonging to Natural, or Ethnic Religious Minorities 1992; Declaration of the Principles of International Cultural Co-operation 1966; Cairo Declaration of Human Rights 1990; Arab Charter on Human Rights 1994; African Charter on Human Rights 1981 and the Declaration on Cultural Diversity 1998.[252]

The role of a declaratory instrument is to make a statement of intention that the signing parties agree to abide by the principles of the declaration. The success or not of that instrument is much dependent upon the actions of the signatory states. I have shown the success of the 1960 Declaration, however, in examining the Arab Charter of Human Rights, we see the complete opposite.

The Arab Charter

Despite Arab and African nations, declaring in principle to the spirit of the Universal Declaration of Human Rights, the practical effect of imposition of those rights upon their respective cultures has fallen far short of the 1948 Declaration. The difficulty is as a result of attempting to assimilate western cultural concepts of human rights, which are rights completely foreign to their own respective cultures.

The Arab Charter on Human Rights 1994 – The Divide Between Western and Arab Cultures

Despite the adoption by the Arab League,[253] of the Arab Charter on Human Rights in 1994, the declaratory instrument still seeks ratification, today.[254] In 2001, steps were taken by the League to hasten this process.[255] The difficulty in Arab States to recognise this apparent universal declaratory instrument, is abundantly clear. The fundamental reason is because it is not compatible with, nor recognisable to rights, which exist in Arab culture, for their cultural principle is dominated by the theological constituent of Islam and heavily influenced by the historical constituent, in past and present conflict with Israel. The struggle indeed, is to find the common ground that exists in the gulf of divide between the 1948 Declaration and the Arab Charter. One such example is the general normative conflict between human rights and the practices of Islam. If the Charter is to succeed, for it cannot in its present form, it will have to be accordingly amended to reflect the apparent universality of the 1948 Declaration. This would mean the concession by the Arab League to surrender entirely to the 1948 Declaration. I, having already declared the 1948 instrument to be of western cultural construct see any concession by the Arab League, to be an indication of movement by Arab culture, to assimilate with western cultural values. The ten years that have past since the inception of the Arab Charter have shown unsuccessful attempts to reconcile the divide between the two instruments. I suggest they are irreconcilable, for Arab culture in its present form, cannot capitulate to a western cultural ideology, through the peace and safe haven of collective cultural relativist negotiation, within the United Nations. The United States recognises this and has embarked upon, as we presently readily see, the espousing of its culturally imperialistic ideology through military force. Arab culture has little option but eventually to submit to the western cultural construct of human rights, after it has been defeated.[256]

The construction of the Charter raises more questions than it answers, for it is in certain respects not a mirror image of the 1948 Declaration and in others it secures certain values akin only to Arab culture. I shall now set out how this is. Firstly, the preamble and Article 1[257] condemns Zionism, a digression of political nature, obscuring the true nature and purpose of the Charter, if it were to be based on the 1948 instrument. Secondly, a supplementary paragraph insertion at Article 2, strips the 1948 Declaration of the principle of non discrimination on the grounds of sex, as it declares men and women to be only equal in human dignity, but to be bound by the shari 'a law in respect to their dealings with each other. Lastly, the Charter has also failed to recognise the following human right provisions, otherwise declared in the 1948 instrument:

- The right not to be held in slavery or servitude.
- The absolute prohibition of the death penalty for: minors, the mentally ill, political crimes.
- The abolition of the death penalty.
- Freedom of religion, in all its components, including the right to adopt the religion of one's choice.
- Freedom of expression.
- Right to Life.
- Prohibition of torture and inhumane treatment.
- Right to a fair trial.

Conclusions:

It was my intention at the outset, to interrogate the role and impact of the instruments, processes and procedures of International Criminal

Justice and how they enforce human rights. It was important to make a preliminary examination of human rights concepts and how such noble ideals first came to the human mind and will. I began with the foundation of law, found in philosophy and with a discussion on the theory of knowledge. It was necessary to do this because human rights as a concept is acquired through knowledge, of it and for it. I embarked on a discussion of the two established views of knowledge. I demonstrated that knowledge had been the subject of much debate since the ancient Greeks. Drawing upon the teachings of Plato, Socrates, Aristotle and much later Rorty and Locke, I showed that one view of it to be in existence as a state of nature and that the acquisition of human rights knowledge was the discovery of these rights as laws of nature. Human rights belonged amongst all natural laws, detached from mankind, but yet still relevant and applicable to him. This detachment I considered to be objective in nature for these laws were not tainted by the views, opinions or the subjectivity of men's thoughts. I then considered the second view, that human rights was not objective, that in fact it was created and moulded into a set of rights by the subjectivity of men. To support this view, I specifically examined Immanuel Kant's thoughts and found his work somewhat enlightening, for he believed that human rights were the product of man himself and really did not exist as a product of nature; that they were subjectively driven and ultimately were formed within a cultural class and progressed in development according to the progression of that particular culture. Further, I found the work of Michael Foucault equally of assistance, in understanding how knowledge and in this case, human rights knowledge could be held as an instrument of power. This allowed knowledge to become hardened, not as a simple piece of information, but more so an ideology upon which a culture would defend its values, traditions and beliefs. More so Alan Rosenboum's identification of four principle influences which impact upon human rights and Jerome Shestack's observation that human rights differs between cultures.

I was able to deduce from the collection of writings that knowledge, or human rights knowledge was and is created within a cultural class. This class is distinguishable from any other by its own value systems, traditions and beliefs, however, the commonality between each culture was the foundation of four guiding principles, its: ethics, theology, politics and history, even though the substance of these principles varied from culture to culture. A cultural class that had the ability to use its knowledge to the best of its ability was in a position to gain strength and power over other cultures. Having acquired a degree of power, it had one of two choices, either to ideologies it and impose knowledge upon other cultures, or to respect the differing interpretations of knowledge, within other cultures and to find common ground, so as to elevate such knowledge to a mutually acceptable objective level. I reconciled the first path, with the well-known concept of cultural imperialism and the second with that of cultural relativism.

Having established that knowledge, in particular human rights knowledge differed from culture to culture I set about supporting this assumption with reference to three cultural classes: Western, Asian and Arab-African. I demonstrated that each's view on human rights was very different, for the latter two classes saw such rights as duties between man, and following the strength in their foundation of the theological principle, and God. In showing these differences I was able to establish that the prevalent human rights view of rights between men, was of western cultural construction and I ventured to reveal was a vehicle used by culturally imperialist states, to secure control over others and that those states opposed to such control, resisted vigorously, by collective effort to neutralise the force of the cultural imperialist pressure.

In this next volume I shall continue to support this set of assumptions, by investigating the historical construct and current state of global institutions, namely the United Nations, The International Criminal Courts for the former Yugoslavia and Rwanda, as well as the now fully functioning International Criminal Court; as empirical foundation of the *cultural principle* in situ.

Bibliography

Anthony Davies

Works cited

S. Palmer, *Arbitrary detention in Guantanamo Bay: legal limbo in the land of the free,* Cambridge Law Journal, 2003

J. Steyn, *Guantanamo Bay: the legal black hole,* International & Comparative Law Quarterly, 2004

S. Sayeed, *Guantanamo Bay – five years on,* Journal of Immigration Asylum and Nationality Law, 2007

B. Tittemore, *Guantanamo Bay and the precautionary measures of the Inter-American Commission on Human Rights: a case for international oversight in the struggle against terrorism,* Human Rights Law Review, 2006

Cases cited

Rasul v Bush

John Does Nos. 1 – 570 v Bush

Hamdan v Rumsfeld

Boumediene v Bush

R (on the application of Abbasi) v Secretary of State for Foreign and Commonwealth Affairs

R (on the application of Al-Rawi) v Secretary of State for Foreign and Commonwealth Affairs

Legislation cited

The Geneva Convention

The European Convention on Human Rights

The Magna Carta

The Human Rights Act 1998

The Detainee Treatment Act 2005 (USA)

The Military Commissions Act 2006 (USA)

The Uniform Code of Military Justice

Electronic resources cited

www.icrc.org

www.europa.eu

www.un.org

www.bbc.co.uk

www.timesonline.co.uk

www.guardian.co.uk

www.gwu.edu

www.icrc.org

Frederick Motson

Works Cited

B. Barber, *'Jihad vs. McWorld'* in *Atlantic Monthly*, 1992

B. Barber, *'Beyond Jihad vs McWorld'* in *The Nation*, January 2002

P. Berger and T. Luckmann, *The Social Construction of Reality*, (Penguin, 1967)

Speech by President G. W. Bush to Congress, September 11th 2001

Address to the Nation, President G.W. Bush, September 11th 2006

N. Chomsky, *'The New War Against Terror'*, in Genest, *Conflict and Cooperation 2ⁿᵈ Edition*, (Thomson, 2004)

C. Combs, *Terrorism in the 21ˢᵗ Century*, (Prentice Hall, 2003)

M. Crenshaw *'The Causes of Terrorism'* in Kegley, *The New Global Terrorism* (2003, Prentice Hall)

M. Crenshaw *'Why is America the Primary Target?'* in Kegley, *The New Global Terrorism* (2003, Prentice Hall)

M. Doyle *"Kant, Liberal Legacies, and Foreign Affairs"* in *Philosophy and Public Affairs* (Vol. 12, No. 3. (Summer, 1983)): 205-235.

D. Druckman, 'Group Attachments in Negotiation and Collective Action' *International Negotiation 11*, 2006

'Second Thoughts about the Promised Land', *The Economist*, January 13ᵗʰ 2007

'The Meaning of Freedom', *The Economist*, May 10ᵗʰ 2007

S. Feshbach, 'Psychology, human violence and the search for peace' *Journal of Social Issues 46*

F. Fukuyama, *The End of History and the Last Man* (Penguin, 1992)

F. Fukuyama, *'The West has won: Radical Islam can't beat democracy and capitalism. We're still at the end of history'* in Genest, *Conflict and Cooperation 2ⁿᵈ Edition*, (Thomson, 2004)

A. Gramsci, *Selections from the Prison Notebooks*, (Lawrence and Wishart, 1971)

H. Grotius, *On The Law of War and Peace*, (1625)

J. Habermas, *The Structural Transformation of the Public Sphere*, (MiT Press, 1989)

I. Hacking, *The Social Construction of What?*, (Harvard, 2000)

N. Hickey, 'Gaining the Media's Attention' in *The Struggle Against Terrorism* (New York, 1977)

J. Hobson, *Imperialism: A Study* (1902)

The Intelligence and Security Committee Report into the London Terrorist Attacks, May 2006

B. Jenkins, *'The Changing Characteristics of Twenty-First Century Global Terrorism'* in Kegley, *The New Global Terrorism* (2003, Prentice Hall)

I. Kant, *Perpetual Peace: A Philosophical Sketch,* (1795)

R. Keohane, *'The Globalization of Informal Violence, Theories of World Politics,* and *"the Liberalism of Fear"* in Genest, *Conflict and Cooperation 2nd Edition,* (Thomson, 2004)

Speech by Dr Henry Kissinger, *'Foreign Policy in the Age of Terrorism',* made to Center for Policy Studies, October 31st 2001

M. Klare, 'The New Face of Combat: Terrorism and Irregular Warfare in the 21st Century' in Kegley, *The New Global Terrorism* (2003, Prentice Hall)

B. Lewis, *'The Roots of Muslim Rage'* in Kegley, *The New Global Terrorism* (2003, Prentice Hall)

A. Linklater, *Dialogic Politics and the Civilising Process* in *Review of International Studies* (Cambridge University Press, 2005) p141-154

H.J. Morgenthau, *Politics Among Nations,* (McGraw Hill, 1993)

J.S. Nye Jr, *Understanding International Conflicts,* (Addison-Wesley, 1993)

J. Starr *'Water wars'* in *Foreign Policy* 82 (Spring 1991): 17-36

J. Steans & L. Pettiford, *Introduction to International Relations 2nd Edition,* (Pearson Longman, 2005)

K. Waltz. *'Structural Realism After the Cold War'* in *International Security* (2000)

K. Waltz, *The Origins of War in Neo-Realist Theory* in *The Journal of Interdisciplinary History,* Vol 18 No 4 (Spring 1998)

P. Wilkinson *'Why Modern Terrorism?'* in Kegley, *The New Global Terrorism* (2003, Prentice Hall)

P. Williams, D. Goldstein & J. Shafritz, *Classic Readings and Contemporary Debates in International Relations 3rd Edition,* (Thomson-Wadworth, 2006)

B. Woodward, *State of Denial* (Simon & Schuster, 2006)

Electronic resources cited

www.bbc.co.uk

www.gallup-international.com

www.guardian.co.uk

www.ics.leeds.ac.uk

www.independent.co.uk

www.prohijab.net

www.theatlantic.com

www.washingtonpost.com

Matthew Proud

Works cited

Freedom House, *Freedom of the Press 2008- Hong Kong*, 29 April 2008

Human Rights Watch, *World Report 2008*. (Seven Stories Press, New York, 2008)

Matthew 11:16: Richard G. Moulton (ed) Richard G. Moulton (ed), *The Modern Reader's Bible*. (New York: Macmillan, 1918)

P.S.N. Lee and L.L. Chu, *Inherent Dependence on Power: Hong Kong Press in Political Transition*. Edited by Sing Ming, Hong Kong Government and Politics (Oxford Press, Oxford New York, 2003)

S. Ming (ed), Hong Kong Government and Politics (Oxford Press, Oxford New York, 2003)

Tung Chee, Interview with the United Press International. Date 22nd May 2001

US Department of State website, *Hong Kong Falun Gong Practitioner(s) Denied Entry*. Date 27th June 2007.

D. Weisenhaus, *Hong Kong Media Law* (Hong Kong University Press, Hong Kong, 2007)

Cases cited

Handyside v United Kingdom (5493/72) [1976] ECHR 5 (1976)

Observer and Guardian v United Kingdom (1991) 14 EHRR 153

Palko v. State of Connecticut, 302 U.S. 319

R v Londonderry (1881) 28 LF Fr. 440

Secretary for Justice v Apple Daily Ltd & Another [2000] 2 HKLRD 704

Sunday Times v United Kingdom (No 2) [1991] IIHRL 70 (1991)

Legislation cited

Convention for the Protection of Human Rights and Fundamental Freedoms (European Convention on Human Rights) 1950

Hong Kong Bill of Rights Ordinance 1991, Part III

Electronic resources cited

www.bbc.co.uk

www.falunhr.org

www.faluninfo.net

www.iht.com

www.nytimes.com

www.state.gov

www.unhcr.org

Dinesh Rajp

Works cited

H. Ando and O. Minear, *The Tokyo War Crimes Trial*, (University Press, Amsterdam, 1979)

I. Brownlie and G.S. Goodwin-Gill, *Basic Documents on Human Rights,* (Oxford University Press, Oxford, 2002)

R. Clayton and H. Tomlinson, *The Law of Human Rights*, (Oxford University Press, Oxford, 2000)

D. Davidson, *Inquiries into Truth and Interpretation* (Oxford University Press, Oxford, 1984)

A.V. Dicey, *Introduction to the Study of the Law of the Constitution*, (Liberty Fund, Indianapolis, 1982)

J. Donnelly, 'International Human Rights: A Regime Analysis', *International Organisation* 40 (3): 599-642.

R. Dworkin, *Taking Rights Seriously*, (Duckworth, London, 1978)

O. Elias, 'The nature of the subjective element in customary international law.' *International and Comparative Law Quarterly* Vol. 44, 1995, p 501.

Dr. Erhard, Speech at meeting of lawyers in Munich on 2nd June 1948, originally published in: *Suddeutsche Juristen-Zeitung*, (July 1948) Volume III, No 7, Columns 358-68.

M. Foucault: *The Archaeology of Knowledge* (Routledge, an imprint by Taylor and Francis Books, 2002)

W. Hohfeld, *Fundamental Legal Conceptions as applied in Judicial Reasoning* (Yale University Press, Yale, 1919)

W. James, *Pragmatism* (Hackett, Indianapolis, 1981)

I. Kant, *Critique of Practical Reason* (1788) (Cambridge University Press, Cambridge, 1998)

I. Kant, *Critique of Pure Reason* (Hackett Publishing, London 1999)

I. Kant, *Metaphysics of Ethics* (1797) (Cambridge University Press, Cambridge, 1998)

I. Kant, *Perpetual Peace and Other Essays* (Hackett Publishing, London, 1983)

E. Kemanka and A. E.-S. Tay (eds), *Human Rights*, (Oxford University Press, Oxford, 1978)

J. Locke, *Two Treaties of Government* (Thomas P. Peardon ed.) (Library of Liberal Arts, New York, 1952)

M. Marrus, *The Nuremberg War Crimes Trial of 1945-6: A Documentary History (Bedford Series in History and Culture)* (Palgrave Macmillan, London, 1997)

R. Nozick, *Anarchy State and Utopia,* (Blackwell, London, 1974)

J. Raz, *The Morality of Freedom,* (Clarendon Press, Cambridge, 1986)

R. Rorty, *Objectivity, Relativism and Truth* (Cambridge University Press, Cambridge, 1991)

R. Rorty, *Philosophy and The Mirror of Nature* (Princeton Paperbacks, Princeton University Press, 1979)

A. Rosenbaum, *The Philosophy of Human Rights-International Perspectives* (Aldwych Press, London, 1981)

C. Schlesinger, *Act of Creation – The Founding of the United Nations,* (Westview Press, New York, 2003)

J.J. Shestack, *The Jurisprudence of Human Rights,* in T. Meron (ed). Human Rights in International Law, (Oxford University Press, Oxford, 1984) pp 69-113

J.J. Shestack, The Philosophic Foundations of Human Rights, 20 *Human Rights Quarterly,* 228 (1998)

H.J. Steiner, 'Securing Human Rights: The First Half of the Universal Declaration of Human Rights' (*Harvard Magazine, Harvard September – October 1998*) p 45.

H.J. Steiner and P. Alston, *International Human Rights in Context - Law, Politics Morals,* (Oxford University Press, Oxford, 2000)

Time Magazine, 20th May 1946, p 24

R.J. Vincent, *Human Rights in International Relations,* (Cambridge University Press, Cambridge, 1986)

K. Waltz, *Theory of International Politics,* (Addison – Wessley, Massachusetts, 1979)

R. Woetzel, *The Nuremburg Trials Against the Major War Criminals and International Law,* (Stevens and Sas, London, 1962)

Cases cited

Ex parte Quirin, 317 U.S. 1 (1942)

Southern Pacific Co. v Jensen (1917) 244 US 205.222.61 Led 1086. 1101, 37 S Ct 524.

Electronic resources cited

www.courts.go.jp/english

www.isop.ucla.edu

www.japan-guide.com

www.lebaneseforces.com

www.trumanlibrary.org

www.un.org

www.unhchr.ch

www.yale.edu/lawweb/

(Endnotes)

1   Article 3 of Convention III relative to the Treatment of Prisoners of War. Geneva, 12 August 1949.

2   Memo from General Counsel of the Department of Defence, Subject: Counter Resistance Techniques, dated November 27, 2002

3   Ibid, hand written on front page

4   Of 1215, England

5   Oxford Dictionary of Law

6   542 US 466 (2004)

7   Ibid

8   Ibid

9   Civil Action No. 05-CV-0313 (CKK)

10   Detainee Treatment Act 2005, Title X, Sec. 1005, Procedures for Status Review of Detainees Outside the United States

11   126 S.Ct. 2749 (2006)

12   Ibid

13   Sadat Sayeed, *Guantanamo Bay – five years on,* Journal of Immigration Asylum and National Law, 2007

14   553 U.S. ___ (2008)

15   [2002] EWCA Civ 1598

16   [2008] Q.B. 289

17   2006 ICRC Annual Report, Washington (Regional)

18   2007 ICRC Annual Report, Washington (Regional)

19   *Amicus Curiae* Brief of 383 United Kingdom and European Parliamentarians in Support of Petitioners

20   This was the final death toll excluding the hijackers and around thirty people missing, presumed dead, as reported by the BBC, CNN and other major news outlets – some sources differ slightly on these figures.

21   On 11th March 2004 191 people died as a result of the bombing of four commuter trains in Madrid by Al-Qaeda operatives.

22   52 people were killed by bomb attacks on Underground trains and

buses on July 7th 2005 in London. The four perpetrators of the attack were all British citizens, born and raised in England.

23   Jenkins sees traditional 20th Century terrorism as "aimed at the people watching, not at the actual victims. Terrorism is theater". Source: Brian Jenkins, 'The Changing Characteristics of Twenty-First Century Global Terrorism' in Kegley, *The New Global Terrorism* (2003, Prentice Hall).

24   Many see Thucydides' *The History of the Peloponnesian War* as the first work to contain recognisable realist principles, particularly the 'balance of power' between states.

25   I.e. 'soldiers' in the traditional or legal sense – while many terrorists claim to be soldiers of a cause or faith, their actions are well outside the scope of methods of war recognised as legitimate by the international community of states.

26   Speech by President Bush to Congress, September 11th 2001

27   Speech by Dr Henry Kissinger, *'Foreign Policy in the Age of Terrorism'*, made to Center for Policy Studies, October 31st 2001 (available at http://ics. leeds.ac.uk/papers/pmt/exhibits/817/kissinger.pdf)

28   In his book *State of Denial* (Simon & Schuster, 2006) and writing for the Washington Post (http://www.washingtonpost.com/wp-dyn/content/ article/2006/09/30/AR2006093000293_pf.html) Bob Woodward alleges that "A powerful, largely invisible influence on Bush's Iraq policy was former secretary of state Kissinger."Of the outside people that I talk to in this job," Vice President Cheney told me in the summer of 2005, "I probably talk to Henry Kissinger more than I talk to anybody else"...The president also met privately with Kissinger every couple of months, making him the most regular and frequent outside adviser to Bush on foreign affairs. "

29   Cindy Combs, *Terrorism in the 21st Century*, (Prentice Hall, 2003) p1

30   This argument has been made in numerous books and articles by Waltz. *'Structural Realism After the Cold War'* in *International Security* (2000) and *The Origins of War in Neo-Realist Theory* in *The Journal of Interdisciplinary History*, Vol 18 No 4 (Spring 1998) are two prime examples

31   "The contingent elements of personality, prejudice, and subjective preference, and of all the weakness of intellect and will which flesh is heir to, are bound to deflect foreign policies from their rational course" Hans J Morgenthau, *Politics Among Nations*, (McGraw Hill, 1993)

32   Cindy Combs, *Terrorism in the 21st Century*, (Prentice Hall, 2003) p26

33   As reported in The Intelligence and Security Committee Report into the London Terrorist Attacks, published May 2006 p12

34   Robert O Keohane, *'The Globalization of Informal Violence, Theories of*

World Politics, and *"the Liberalism of Fear"* in Genest, *Conflict and Cooperation 2nd Edition*, (Thomson, 2004)

35   Seen as the founder of modern economic liberalism, Smith's most famous work is his *Wealth of Nations*

36   A phrase coined by Huntington (see below) but in increasingly popular usage, for example by President Bush in his Address to the Nation commemorating the 5th anniversary of 9/11 (Source of transcript: http://www. washingtonpost.com/wp-dyn/content/article/2006/09/11/AR2006091100775. html)

37   · "Water security will soon rank with military security in the war rooms of defence ministries....One of Israel's strategic concerns in granting territory to the Palestinians is the future of the Yarkon/Taninim mountain aquifer that lies beneath" Starr, J. R. 1991. 'Water wars' in *Foreign Policy* 82 (Spring): 17-36

38   Originated in Immanuel Kant, *Perpetual Peace: A Philosophical Sketch,* (1795): "The First Definitive Article For a Perpetual Peace – The Civil Constitution of Every State Should be Republican...If the consent of the citizens is required in order to decide that war should be declared (and in this constitution it cannot but be the case) nothing is more natural than that they would be very cautious in commencing such a poor game"
For a modern interpretation see Doyle, Michael W. "Kant, Liberal Legacies, and Foreign Affairs" in *Philosophy and Public Affairs* (Vol. 12, No. 3. (Summer, 1983)): 205-235.

39   Cindy Combs, *Terrorism in the 21st Century*, (Prentice Hall, 2003) p85

40   Hugo Grotius, *On The Law of War and Peace,* (1625)

41   Immanuel Kant, *Perpetual Peace: A Philosophical Sketch,* (1795): "The Second Definitive Article For a Perpetual Peace – The Law Of Nations Shall be Founded on a Federation of Free States".

42   See *'The Meaning of Freedom'*, The Economist, 10/5/07 and http:// www.prohijab.net/english/tunis-hijab-news3.htm

43   For example in the Gallup poll taken prior to the invasion of Iraq (available at www.gallup-international.com) 33% of American, 9% of German and 10% of British respondents were in favour of unilateral action, however a further 34% of American, 39% of German and 39% of British respondents said they would support the war if it was sanctioned by the UN.

44   Robert O Keohane, *'The Globalization of Informal Violence, Theories of World Politics, and "the Liberalism of Fear"* in Genest, *Conflict and Cooperation 2nd Edition*, (Thomson, 2004)

45   Joseph S Nye Jr, *Understanding International Conflicts*, (Addison-Wesley, 1993)

46   In 2004, the European Union and the US agreed that airlines leaving

Europe for the US would provide a range of information about every passenger. In May 2006 the European Court of Justice ruled that it had not been given a suitable legal foundation in European law and talks to renew the agreement have since collapsed

47   Steans & Pettiford, *Introduction to International Relations 2nd Edition*, (Pearson Longman, 2005)

48   Williams, Goldstein & Shafritz, *Classic Readings and Contemporary Debates in International Relations 3rd Edition,* (Thomson-Wadworth, 2006)

49   Genest, *Conflict and Cooperation 2nd Edition*, (Thomson, 2004)

50   John Hobson, *Imperialism: A Study* (1902)

51   Noam Chomsky, *'The New War Against Terror'*, (as published in Genest, *Conflict and Cooperation 2nd Edition*, (Thomson, 2004)

52   Michael Klare, 'The New Face of Combat: Terrorism and Irregular Warfare in the 21st Century' in Kegley, *The New Global Terrorism* (2003, Prentice Hall)

53   Cindy Combs, *Terrorism in the 21st Century*, (Prentice Hall, 2003) p81

54   It should be noted that realists such as Kissinger still see stateless terrorist organisations as in collusion with certain nations, claiming that "in the Middle East there is a kind of tacit agreement between these 'cells' and the government in which the government tolerates these cells so long as they do not direct their actions against the countries in which they are located"

55   Antonio Gramsci, *Selections from the Prison Notebooks*, (Lawrence and Wishart, 1971)

56   Benjamin Barber, *'Jihad vs. McWorld'* in *Atlantic Monthly*, 1992 http://www.theatlantic.com/politics/foreign/barberf.htm.

57   Steans & Pettiford, *Introduction to International Relations 2nd Edition*, (Pearson Longman, 2005) p121

58   Jürgen Habermas, *The Structural Transformation of the Public Sphere,* (MiT Press, 1989)

59   In this extreme form – it is not suggested that any rational interpretation of Islamic doctrine, however strict, suggests anything of the sort.

60   Andrew Linklater, *Dialogic Politics and the Civilising Process* in *Review of International Studies* (Cambridge University Press, 2005) p141-154
61   Benjamin Barber, *'Jihad vs McWorld'* in *Atlantic Monthly*, 1992

62   Francis Fukuyama, *The End of History and the Last Man* (Penguin, 1992)

63   Ian Hacking, *The Social Construction of What?*, (Harvard, 2000)

64   Cindy Combs, *Terrorism in the 21st Century*, (Prentice Hall, 2003) p116

65   Quoted in Neil Hickey, 'Gaining the Media's Attention' in *The Struggle Against Terrorism* (New York, 1977)

66   In Britain voter turnout has dropped well below the normal historical range of between 70-90% to around 60%. In the United States the decline began in the 1960s, although the 2004 election saw a sharp increase in turnout, particularly among the young. This is perhaps explained by the polemic nature of the election and the Bush presidency

67   Cindy Combs, *Terrorism in the 21st Century*, (Prentice Hall, 2003) p61

68   Ibid., p150

69   *'The Mystery of Sid'*, BBC News, http://news.bbc.co.uk/1/hi/magazine/4354858.stm

70   As reported in The Intelligence and Security Committee Report into the London Terrorist Attacks, May 2006 p12

71   Berger and Luckmann, *The Social Construction of Reality*, (Penguin, 1967)

72   Ibid., p158

73   Ibid., p165

74   Martha Crenshaw 'The Causes of Terrorism' in Kegley, *The New Global Terrorism* (2003, Prentice Hall)

75   Simone de Beauvoir was a famous 20th Century philosopher, perhaps known for her oft-quoted line "One is not born, but rather becomes a woman", referring to the construction of 'gender'.

76   Francis Fukuyama, *'The West has won: Radical Islam can't beat democracy and capitalism. We're still at the end of history'* (as published in Genest, *Conflict and Cooperation 2nd Edition*, (Thomson, 2004))

77   Benjamin Barber, *'Beyond Jihad vs McWorld'* in *The Nation*, January 2002

78   Ian Hacking, *The Social Construction of What?*, (Harvard, 2000)

79   The Guardian, *'Cornish militants rise again – and this time they're targeting celebrity chefs'*, 14/06/07

80   Noam Chomsky, *'The New War Against Terror'*, (as published in Genest, *Conflict and Cooperation 2nd Edition*, (Thomson, 2004)

81   For example see *'Afghan Success in the New 'Great Game'*, BBC News, 11/10/04 http://news.bbc.co.uk/1/hi/world/south_asia/3733454.stm

82   Egypt's Presidential elections are seen by those both within

the country and international observers as firmly rigged in favour of the government – see for example http://news.independent.co.uk/world/middle_east/article310985.ece on the 2005 elections

83   Official EU observers branded the 2007 Nigerian elections as "far short of basic international and regional standards...[which] cannot be considered to have been credible...marred by poor organisation, lack of essential transparency, widespread procedural irregularities, significant evidence of fraud, particularly during the result collation process, voter disenfranchisement at different stages of the process, and lack of equal conditions for contestants." (From official EU Press Release)

84   In 1933 Hitler's NSDAP (Nazi) Party and its allies the DVNP won 340 of 647 seats, giving it an overall majority.

85   Hamas won 44.45% of votes, while Fatah won 41.43%, but the use of the 'first past the post' system to fill half the seats gave Hamas an overall majority with 56% of seats in the Legislative Council.

86   'Hegemony' in this context is meant in a Gramscian cultural sense – areas such as Helmland Province in Afghanistan are nominally under the control of the relatively liberal Afghan government in Kabul rather than the Taleban, but even in areas where the Taleban do not continue to terrorise the local population many citizens practice an extremely conservative if not fanatical form of Islam.

87   Cindy Combs, *Terrorism in the 21st Century*, (Prentice Hall, 2003) p277

88   Paul Wilkinson 'Why Modern Terrorism?' in Kegley, *The New Global Terrorism* (2003, Prentice Hall)

89   Martha Crenshaw 'Why is America the Primary Target?' in Kegley

90   Bernard Lewis, 'The Roots of Muslim Rage' in Kegley

91   Martha Crenshaw 'The Causes of Terrorism' in Kegley

92   Feshback identified 'patriotic' identities as "an emotional attachment to one's own group without feelings of superiority or denigration of other groups or countries... [whereas 'nationalism'] emphasizes a kind of moral and material superiority for one's own group or country". See Seymour Feshbach, 'Psychology, human violence and the search for peace' *Journal of Social Issues 46* and Daniel Druckman, 'Group Attachments in Negotiation and Collective Action' *International Negotiation 11,* 2006

93   The BBC reported that on 2nd May 2006 "More than a million" immigrants in the United States protested against tough new anti-immigration laws which would try to reduce the number of illegal aliens in the country. Source: http://news.bbc.co.uk/1/hi/world/americas/4961734.stm

94   'Second Thoughts about the Promised Land', *The Economist,* January 13th 2007

95   Berger and Luckmann, *The Social Construction of Reality*, (Penguin, 1967) p186

96   Article 10 of the European Convention on Human Rights

97   ibid

98   Interview with the United Press International, date 22 May 2001

99   US Department of State, *Hong Kong Falun Gong Practitioner(s) Denied Entry*. Date 27th June 2007. Available on line at www.state.gov/r/pa/prs/ps/2007/jun/87489.htm,

100   140 Taiwanese practitioners blocked from entering Hong Kong. Source:www.faluninfo.net/article/604/

101   Hong Kong Bill of Rights Ordinance 1991, Part III

102   Palko v. State of Connecticut, 302 U.S. 319: *"Freedom of thought... is the matrix, the indispensable condition, of nearly every other form of freedom. With rare aberrations a pervasive recognition of this truth can be traced in our history, political and legal."*

103   Matthew 11:16: *Richard G. Moulton (ed) Richard G. Moulton (ed), The Modern Reader's Bible. (New York: Macmillan, 1918)*

104   BBC World News: *Hong Kong tries Falun Gong members,* 17th June 2002. Online at http://news.bbc.co.uk/1/hi/world/asia-pacific/2049030.stm

105   28 LF Fr. 440

106   Source: http://query.nytimes.com/gst/fullpage.html?res=9907E0D615 3AF931A15754C0A9679C8B63

107   O'Brian J, in *R v Londonderry (1881)*

108   Source: http://www.falunhr.org/index.php?option=com_frontpage&Itemid=1

109   US Department of State. Available at: www.state.gov/g/drl/rls/rm/2005/50110.htm

110   Article 6 of the European Convention on Human Rights

111   *"The Courts of the Hong Kong Special Administrative Region shall exercise judicial power independently, free form any interference."*

112   International Herald Tribune, *Hong Kong reverses Falun Gong convictions.* 6th May 2005. Online at: www.iht.com/articles/2005/05/05/news/hong.php

113   Handyside v United Kingdom (5493/72) [1976] ECHR 5 (1976)

114   Sunday Times v United Kingdom (No 2) [1991] IIHRL 70 (1991)

115   Observer and Guardian v United Kingdom (1991) 14 EHRR 153

116   Article 23 Hong Kong Basic Law

117   Wong, Yiu-Chung, *One Country, Two Systems in Crisis: Hong Kong's Transformation Since the Handover.* (Lexington Books, Oxford, 2004)

118   The Times Higher Education, *The Worlds Top 200 Universities.* Available at: www.timeshighereducation.co.uk/hybrid.asp?typeCode=144

119   Freedom House, *Freedom of the Press 2008- Hong Kong,* 29 April 2008. Online. UNHCR Refworld, available at: http://www.unhcr.org/refworld/docid/4871f60ac.html [accessed 2 September 2008]

120   Doreen Weisenhaus, *Hong Kong Media Law.*(Hong Kong University Press, Hong Kong, 2007) Page 146

121   ibid

122   ibid

123   Secretary for Justice v Apple Daily Ltd & Another [2000] 2 HKLRD 704

124   Human Rights Watch, *World Report 2008.* (Seven Stories Press, New York, 2008) Page 270

125   Sing Ming (ed), Hong Kong Government and Politics (Oxford Press, Oxford New York, 2003) Page 586

126   ibid page 587

127   ibid

128   Freedom House, *Freedom of the Press 2008- Hong Kong,* 29 April 2008. Online. UNHCR Refworld, available at: http://www.unhcr.org/refworld/docid/4871f60ac.html [accessed 2 September 2008]

129   Paul S. N. Lee and Leonard L. Chu, *Inherent Dependence on Power: Hong Kong Press in Political Transition*. Edited by Sing Ming, Hong Kong Government and Politics (Oxford Press, Oxford New York, 2003) Page 591

130   ibid

131   ibid

132   R. Rorty, *Philosophy and The Mirror of Nature* (Princeton Paperbacks, Princeton University Press, 1979) p 136.

133   The word "Epistemology." is a word used in philosophical and scientific circles to mean the same as the "Theory of Knowledge".

134   Supra note 1.
135   Supra note 1.
136   (1724 – 1804), German Philosopher.

137   I. Kant, *Critique of Pure Reason* (Hackett Publishing, London 1999) p 1.

138   I. Kant, *Critique of Practical Reason* (Cambridge University Press, Cambridge, 1979) p 17.

139   A current public philosopher (1931-), noted for his work: *Philosophy and the Mirror of Nature*

(Princeton Paperbacks, Princeton University Press, 1979)

140   R. Rorty, *Philosophy and the Mirror of Nature* (Princeton Paperbacks, Princeton University Press, 1979) p. 137. – The correctness or otherwise of Kant's proposition may explain the evolution of human rights, possibly evolving not as some invisible form, but more so from the subjectivity of individuals or a group of individuals holding the same or similar view. I shall expand upon this in later chapters.

141   Supra note 7, p 25.
142   Supra note 7, p 62.
143   I. Kant, *Perpetual Peace and Other Essays* (Hackett Publishing, London, 1983) p 86.

144   Supra note 7, p 89. Kant's *"state of international right"* in modern terms may be interpreted as the body that is the United Nations.. *"The public laws backed by force"* may be interpreted as the force exerted by the United Nations, to implement public international law.

145   Supra note 7. Kant's view was largely influenced by the politics of the time and the prominence of Europe as the major battleground of nations, both in wartime and in peace. Kant's view that this utopian body cannot exist entirely in a utopian state is reflected in certain instances where the United Nations has been impotent to affect international public law. However, the force Kant refers to, may not necessarily be that of a military nature, but may also refer to legal or judicial force. For example, the forming of the International Criminal Courts reflects that international public law can be enforced with effect.

146   Supra note 7, p 86.
147   I. Kant, *Metaphysics of Ethics* (1797) (Cambridge University Press, Cambridge, 1998) and *Critique of Practical Reason* (1788) (Cambridge University Press, Cambridge, 1998)

148   Supra note 7, p 87.
149   Supra note 7, p 94.
150   Supra note 7, p 98.
151   Supra note 9, p 12.
152   Supra note 9, p 155-156.
153   Supra note 9, chapter VIII.
154   Supra note 9, chapter VIII. The writer's general overview of this chapter expressed in this paragraph.

155   Supra note 9, p 357.

156   Supra note 9, p 362.

157   Supra note 9, p 354. Rorty refers to these sciences as *'Naturwissenschaft'* and *'Geistewissenschaft'*.

158   Supra note 9, p 362.

159   Supra note 9, p 363.

160   Supra note 9, p 23.

161   Supra note 9, p 363.

162   R. Rorty, *Objectivity, Relativism and Truth* (Cambridge University Press, Cambridge, 1991) p 23.

163   Donald Davidson, *Inquiries into Truth and Interpretation* (Oxford University Press, Oxford, 1984)

164   William James, *Pragmatism* (Hackett, Indianapolis, 1981)

165   Ibid note 33.

166   Supra note 33, p 126.

167   As quoted in an unpublished letter by Clare O'Farrell, to the Times Literary Supplement, February 2002.

168   M. Foucault: *The Archaeology of Knowledge* (Routledge, an imprint by Taylor and Francis Books, May 2002) p 186.

169   Source: http://sipi.usc.edu/~knayak/quotes.html

170   Holmes, J., (dissenting) *Southern Pacific Co. v Jensen* (1917) 244 US 205.222.61 Led 1086. 1101, 37 S Ct 524.

171   Dicey, A.V. *Introduction to the Study of the Law of the Constitution*, (Indianapolis: Liberty Fund, 1982).

172   UNESCO – Universal Declaration on Cultural Diversity, para. 5, adopted by the 31st Session of the General Conference of UNESCO, Paris, 2 November 2001. This echoes the definition provided at: The World Conference on Cultural Policies (MONDIACULT, Mexico City, 1982); The World Commission on Culture and Development (Our Creative Diversity) 1995; and The Intergovernmental Conference on Cultural Policies for Development (Stockholm) 1998.

173   Jerome J. Shestack, The Philosophic Foundations of Human Rights, 20 *Human Rights Quarterly,* 228 (1998).

174   Alan S. Rosenbaum, *The Philosophy of Human Rights-International Perspectives*, (Aldwych Press,

London, 1981).

175   Ibid note 43, p 33. The view of the writers H.L.A. Hart and Aiken.

176   Supra note 43, p 33.

177   Supra note 43, p 34.

178   Supra note 43, p 35-37.

179   A more detailed account of such origin seen at E. Kemanka and A. E.-S. Tay (eds), *Human Rights*,

   (Oxford University Press, Oxford, 1978) chapters I and II; J.J. Shestack, *The Jurisprudence of Human Rights*, in T. Meron (ed). Human Rights in International Law, (Oxford University Press, Oxford, 1984) pp 69-113 and R.J. Vincent, *Human Rights in International Relations*, (Cambridge University Press, Cambridge, 1986) Chapter 2.

180   Article 2. The French Declaration of the Rights of Man and the Citizen 1789.

181   *The Spirit of Laws* (1748).

182   *The Social Contract*.

183   Locke J, *Two Treaties of Government* (Thomas P. Peardon ed.) (Library of Liberal Arts, New York,

   1952).

184   H.J. Steiner and P. Alston, *International Human Rights in Context - Law, Politics Morals*, (Oxford University Press, Oxford, 2000) p 324.

185   Ibid note 53, p 325.
186   By the 13 American Colonies on July 4th 1776.

187   Supra note 53, p 325.
188   August 26, 1789.

189   Supra note 53, p 325.
190   W. Hohfeld, *Fundamental Legal Conceptions as applied in Judicial Reasoning* (Yale University Press, Yale, 1919)

191   Richard Clayton and Hugh Tomlinson, *The Law of Human Rights*, (Oxford University Press, Oxford, 2000) p 20.

192   R. Dworkin, *Taking Rights Seriously*, (Duckworth, London, 1978)

193   Supra note 53, pp 90-94 and 364-368.
194   R. Nozick, *Anarchy State and Utopia,* (Blackwell, London, 1974.)

195   Raz, *The Morality of Freedom,* (Clarendon Press, Cambridge, 1986.)

196   Supra note 60, p 22.
197   Supra note 60, p 22.
198   Supra note 53, pp 387-389.
199   Supra note 53, p 392.
200   The Quar'an, verse 4:34.

201   Ibid Note 69, verse 9:29.

202   J. Donnelly, 'International Human Rights: A Regime Analysis', *International Organisation* 40 (3): 599-642.

203   Kenneth N. Waltz, *Theory of International Politics*, (Addison – Wessley, Massachusetts, 1979) p 67.

204   Ibid note 72.
205   Olufmi Elias, 'The nature of the subjective element in customary international law.' *International and*

Comparative Law Quarterly Vol. 44, 1995, p 501.

206   Ibid note 75, p 509.

207   Supra note 75, p 520.

208   I. Brownlie and G.S. Goodwin-Gill, *Basic Documents on Human Rights,* (Oxford University Press, Oxford, 2002), p. 2-*"Signed on the 26th June 1945, in San Francisco, at the conclusion of the United Nations Conference on International Organisation and came into force on 24th October 1945."*

209   Ibid note 77, p 2.
210   Source: www.un.org/aboutun/history.htm A term first used by United States President Franklin D.

Roosevelt and later used in title at the *Declaration by United Nations* of 1st January 1942, when

representatives of 26 nations pledged their Governments to continue fighting together against the Axis

powers, during World War II.

211   Ibid note 79.
212   C. Schlesinger, *Act of Creation – The Founding of the United Nations*, (Westview Press, New York,

2003) p.15. See also: www.trumanlibrary.org/ww2/stofunio.htm The view of President Truman.

213   Source: www.yale.edu/lawweb/avalon/presiden/inaug.eisen2.htm The view of President Eisenhower.

214   Source: www.un.org/formation.html

215   For example: India which then included Pakistan and Bangladesh, having colonial ties with the United Kingdom; South Africa had strong colonial ties with European states, Holland and the United Kingdom.

216   Michael R. Marrus, *The Nuremberg War Crimes Trial of 1945-6: A Documentary History (Bedford Series in History and Culture*, (Palgrave Macmillan, London, 1997) p 12.

217   Supra note 75, p 505.

218   Supra note 86, p 22.

219   Supra note 86.

220   Supra note 86.

221   Supra note 86.

222   Supra note 86, p 42.

223   Supra note 86, pp 44-47.

224   Robert K. Woetzel, *The Nuremburg Trials Against the major War Criminals and International Law*, (Stevens and Sas, London, 1962) p. 24. Speech read by Dr. Erhard, Minister and President of Bavaria, at the meeting of Lawyers in Munich on 2nd June 1948, originally published in: Suddeutsche Juristen- Zeitung, (July 1948) Volume III, No 7, Columns 358-68.

225   Supra note 86, p 35.

226   For, the Germanic system relied upon the responsibility of the Judge as enquirer, to disseminate key issues and conduct a trial based upon enquiries and mediation of the Judge, as opposed to the Anglo – Saxon concept of the pitting of wits between Prosecution and Defence, interlocked as adversaries in battle, the judge making final judgement.

227   Supra note 94.

228   Supra note 94, p 36. The German Lawyer, Von Otto Kranzbuhler.

229   317 U.S. 1, 46 (1942).

230   *Time Magazine,* 20th May 1946, p 24.

231   Hosoya Ando and Onuma Minear, *The Tokyo War Crimes Trial*, (University Press, Amsterdam, 1979)

    p 38.

232   Supra note 94, p 42. Joseph B. Keenan, Chief Counsel, Tokyo War Crimes Trial.

233   Supra note 94. Prime Minister Tojo Hideki.

234   Source: www.japan-guide.com/e/e2130.html

235   Source: www.isop.ucla.edu/eas/documents/ japan1889meijiconstitution.html

236   Ibid note 105, chapter III and IV of the Constitution.

237   Source: www.oefre.unibe.ch/law/icl/ja0000_.html The current Japanese Constitution.

238   Supra note 105, Article 4.

239   Supra note 105, Article 7.

240   Supra note 105, Article 15.

241   Supra note 105, Article 24.

242   Supra note 105, Article 39.

243   Source: www.courts.go.jp/english/soshikie_1.html.

244   Source: www.lebaneseforces.com/malikabout.asp Charles Malik had been educated, worked and lived

under western cultural influence all his life. Having studied at: the American University of Beirut

(1924); Harvard for a PhD, (1937) and a Professor at various American Universities, he also became

the Lebanese Ambassador to the United States in 1947.

245   Supra note 53, p 150.

246   Supra note 53, p 138. The Soviet Union, South Africa and Saudi Arabia, abstained.

247   Henry Steiner, 'Securing Human Rights: The First Half of the Universal Declaration of Human

Rights' (*Harvard Magazine, Harvard September – October 1998*) p 45.

248   Supra note 53, p 367.

249   Supra note 117.

250   Brownlie and Goodwin-Gill, *Basic Documents on Human Rights*, (Oxford University Press, Oxford

2002) p 25, paragraph 1.

251   Ibid note 120, p 26, paragraph 5.

252   Source: www.un.org

253   A collection of Arabic States, formed shortly after World War II, under the *Alexandria Protocol,*

October 7th 1944 and the *Pact of the League of Arab States*, March 22nd 1945 its objectives at Article

1, declared as being: *"The object of the League will be to control the execution of the agreements*

which the above states will conclude; to hold periodic meetings which will strengthen the relations

between those states; to coordinate their political plans so as to insure their cooperation, and

protect their independence and sovereignty against every aggression by suitable means; and to supervise in a general way the affairs an interests of the Arab countries."

254   Source: http://www.unhchr.ch European Social and Economic Council, written statement, paragraph

1.

255   Ibid note 124. Arab League Resolution 6089 of 12 March 2001.

256   We see this with the United States' invasion of Iraq and its current 'warmongering' with Iran.

257   Source: www.un.org

About the Author

John Tomlinson practiced as a stockbroker with Thomson & McKinnon, a member of the New York Stock Exchange. Having studied the effect of debt on national economies, he set up, and is Chairman of, Oxford Research and Development Corporation Limited which explores the use of equity instruments and the development of equity markets.

Malcolm Sinclair, Earl of Caithness, joined the Thatcher government in 1984. He started as a Whip and Lord in Waiting to The Queen before progressing to Minister of State at, successively, the Home Office, Department of the Environment, the Treasury, the Foreign & Commonwealth Office and the Department of Transport. He was created a Privy Councillor to Her Majesty The Queen in 1990. As a hereditary peer he still takes an active part in politics in Parliament.

Frederick Motson studied Law & Politics at the University of Buckingham, where he achieved the Edgar Palamountain Award for Excellence. A member of Grays Inn, he was called to the Bar in October 2008. He currently teaches Law at the University of Westminster.

After serving for many years in the Royal Navy, Anthony Davies turned his attention to academia; completing his law degree, a Masters in commercial and international law and undertaking the Legal Practice Course. Currently, he is working at a major Oxford-based law firm.

Matthew Proud is an international law specialist who primarily focuses on Human Rights issues in Hong Kong. After completing his Bachelor degree he went on to complete a Masters degree in Law, undertaking empirical research in Hong Kong.

Dinesh Rajp achieved his bachelor's degree and a Master's degree in law at the University of Buckingham. He is currently a lecturer in law at the University of Westminster. His research specialisations lie in human rights and international law.